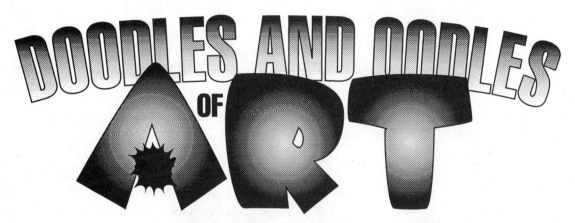

DOODLES AND OODLES OF ART

Hands-On, Process-Oriented Art Experiences from Everyday Materials

Written by Iris Siegler and Kim Torgerson

Illustrated by Chris Nye

When you pick up a brush don't ever ask anyone for help. Because the most wonderful thing about painting is being left alone with your own imagination. I do not paint to get praise from others, but to play a game of endless joy.

—Wang Yani

A Young Painter. By Zheng Zhensun and Alice Low. New York: Scholastic Inc., 1991. A Byron Press/New China Pictures Book. Reprinted by permission of Scholastic Inc.

Teaching & Learning Company

1204 Buchanan St., P.O. Box 10

Carthage, IL 62321

This book is dedicated to all the children who are forever teaching us to go beyond our creative limits and to grow and expand within ourselves

...To our families who have patiently put up with our experimentation and long working hours

...To Nancee McClure who has believed in us

...And to all of you who have attended our workshops and have shown us that we can make a difference! Our energy and enthusiasm is contagious, and you take that back into your schools and classrooms!

Thank you!

This book was developed for the Teaching & Learning Company by The Good Neighbor Press, Inc., Grand Junction, CO.

Cover by The Good Neighbor Press, Inc., Grand Junction, CO.

TABLE OF CONTENTS

And You Thought Joint Compound Was Just for Your Walls!

Something's Fishy . . . But It Doesn't Smell Fishy

Holiday and Gift Section

Recipes

Art is what kids do to survive in an authoritarian society.
                                                                    — Fred Babb

Dear Teacher,

Kim and I got involved in doing art with children because we became frustrated and bored with the everyday art that was being taught at various conferences and workshops. We both knew that we were not into product-oriented art, so we began looking at and exploring various mediums and sharing ideas with one another. I began by doing small "hands-on" workshops. Kim asked me to do a workshop for child development students at the North Idaho College. We found that we worked well together and that creative ideas seemed to flow quite naturally. We began with our Spiney Ball Art, the discovery of drywall joint compound and weather stripping. From that we decided to work together doing hands-on workshops. The excitement and enthusiasm from all the participants was overwhelming. We were hooked. We then applied to do our first really big conference, the *National Association for the Education of Young Children*. Originally we expected 50-100 people at our workshop. Kim had to take the microphone away from me as people began arriving. I kept saying, "I can't believe all these people!" There were 500-600! This is how and why we began the process of "live demonstrations." We have had to utilize this process for the large presentations, but our first love is the "hands-on" workshops because we can work with a room full of enthusiastic, creative teachers, students and parents!

You will find some different and unusual art experiences in this book. We hope they will inspire the creativity within you to go beyond what is here and discover different avenues of creative art. Do not limit the boundaries or materials to those we have listed. We have not given specific ages for these art experiences because we feel that you best know the capabilities of your children and yourself. Some art projects require close supervision and some do not. You must judge that for yourself.

A creative art program should be available to children on a daily basis. Art is the foundation for many things. It develops self-esteem, logic, prereading skills, hand and eye coordination, science, math, writing and geography. For many, art is a private and individual thing, while others like to verbalize and share their excitement and thoughts.

There is no right or wrong way with "process art." We do have some recommendations, however, that will help make your experiences rewarding and creative. 1) Don't hurry. There must be time to explore and play with the various art mediums. You cannot expect a wonderful experience to emerge if you have only one half hour of art a week. 2) Let art be an outlet to expression. 3) Creative, open-ended art is for everyone. Its purpose is to please no one but the artist. 4) Remember, some of the best art never makes it to paper. It is on the children's hands and faces and in their minds as they explore and think about the process.

Art should be fun and exciting. It should come from many different materials and provide many different experiences. Every classroom should always have paper, markers, scissors, glue, hole punches, staples and tape that are readily available for use.

Within each classroom there are many creative imaginations eagerly waiting to be set free.

Sincerely,

Iris Siegler

Kim Torgerson

Whenever you are doing art with children, please note the materials being used. Some may be inappropriate with very small children – there may be small parts, objects may be sharp, vapors dangerous, etc. You should know the capabilities of your children. Always use common sense, get additional volunteers to help if needed, work in small groups or individually. If you feel uncomfortable using something, then don't use it or find a substitute item that might work. Use extreme caution when needed, and never leave art materials or items out unsupervised if they could pose a threat to a child. Art needs to be fun, creative and safe. PLEASE USE GOOD JUDGEMENT!

STAGES OF ART DEVELOPMENT

We feel it is important to know where a child may be developmentally when you are doing art with them. Since I work with two- and three-year-olds in my preschool program, I spend a good deal of time at the beginning of the school year introducing them to art materials. Many have never held a paintbrush (sad but true), worked with glue, paint or the many other materials, textures and tools that we use in everyday art.

Kim on the other hand, has three-, four- and five-year-olds who have been in preschool and have had more art experiences and are developmentally in the "preschematic" art stage. It's interesting to be aware of the different stages of art development. There are always exceptions.

A. Disordered scribbling – 18 months
- Children make random marks with no visual control.
- Crayons are held in various ways with little control.
- Children enjoy the activity for the sake of novelty.

B. Controlled scribbling – around 2 years
- Child discovers a connection between the crayon in his hand and the mark on the paper.
- Motions vary and scribbles become more elaborate.
- Children have no idea "what" they are drawing; they just enjoy the feel.

C. Naming of scribbling – around 3 to 3½ years
- Children draw with more intent, but their scribbles may not look any different.
- Children are influenced by what they want to draw and believe their drawings look like it!

Adult's Role:
- Offer a variety of tools — wide and skinny crayons, markers, pens and pencils
- Value their work. Post it where they can see it!

D. Preschematic — around 4 to 7 years
- Circular and line forms turn into recognizable "things" and shapes: person, sun, house.
- Usually, around age 5, the first symbol is a person without a torso.
- Children will experiment freely with color. People can be green, trees purple.
- The "base line," or sky and ground, appears in drawings.
- The child's immature-looking figures do not represent how they actually perceive figures.

Adult's Role:
- Never criticize the child's odd choice of color or try to guess what the drawing is. Rather ask open-ended questions like "Tell me about your drawing . . ." or "That's interesting."
- Provide a variety of materials — different papers, pens and markers, scissors, items to glue, tape, etc.
- Allow the child to create freely without adult help or suggestions like "Stay inside the lines."

The Process Is More Important Than the Product!

A special thank-you to Carol Lindsay, head instructor of child development at North Idaho College and Educational Program Director, who helped us with her insight, notes and knowledge on "The Stages of Art Development."

Reprinted with permission from Carol Lindsay.

In the book, *A Young Painter* by Zheng Zhensun and Alice Low (Scholastic Inc., 1991. New York, A Byron Press/New China Picture Book) there is a quote from Wang Yani's father. (Wang Yani is China's extraordinary young artist. She began painting at two and now in her teens, still paints incredible pictures!) Yani's father states, "We should encourage children to think and paint by themselves. Adults should never interfere and do things for them because we do not have the innocent minds children have."

A Young Painter. By Zheng Zhensun and Alice Low. New York: Scholastic Inc., 1991. A Byron Press/New China Pictures Book. Reprinted by permission of Scholastic Inc.

PLUNGER ART

MATERIALS:
Plungers in varying sizes
Tempera paint
Large sheets of butcher paper or construction paper
Flat containers to hold paint (pie tins work well)

PROCESS:
Pour desired tempera paints into containers. Place plungers in paint and then press onto paper. The suction buildup causes the paint to fan out, creating interesting patterns and causing the plunger to stick to the paper. By placing a finger or a flat object under the plunger, the vacuum can then be released.

You can use black paint on white paper for an interesting negative/positive design.

Use a large piece of butcher paper and make wrapping paper. Try seasonal colors of paint or bright primary colors.

Experiment with metallic paint.

Use colored glue instead of the tempera paint. Glitter may be added if desired.

WEATHER STRIPPING PRINTS

MATERIALS:

Cardboard
Adhesive vinyl foam tape (weather stripping)
Tempera paint
Brayers
Flat containers for paint that brayers will easily fit into for rolling

PROCESS:

Cut cardboard into varying shapes. These will become your pattern boards. Fill containers with paint so that the brayers can easily be rolled.

Have children cut the weather stripping and peel off the backing. Press onto the cardboard to make their picture or pattern. For younger children it is easier to pre-cut the weather stripping, and let them peel it and place it on the cardboard.

Roll the brayers in paint and brayer over the pattern board. Place a sheet of paper on top of the pattern board and rub. Lift off the paper and your picture will have transferred its pattern. You can make additional prints with your pattern board or save it as a relief picture.

You can use this technique to make wonderful holiday cards.

Some children love to spell their names with the pieces of weather stripping. Please remember, it will print backwards!

SPINEY BALL ART

MATERIALS:
Rubber dog or cat ball* that can be purchased
  in a pet store
Tempera paint
Paper
Circular plastic tub
Pie tins or bowl for paint

PROCESS:
With the paper already cut to fit the bottom of the circular tub and placed inside, dip the spiney ball in the container of paint and put on the paper. Grasp the sides of the tub and roll the ball around, adding other paint colors as needed.

This is a great hand-and-eye exercise. It takes coordination to get the ball rolling around in a circular motion. When adding other paint colors, they overlap and blend, making an interesting print.

To create a mural, cut out and fit butcher paper into a small, plastic swimming pool. Using many spiney balls, dipped into assorted colors of paint, have a group of children work together to roll and create patterns on the paper. This is a great icebreaker and fun to do on a parent night at your school or center.

We like to cut out black paper and use fluorescent paint. The results are spectacular!

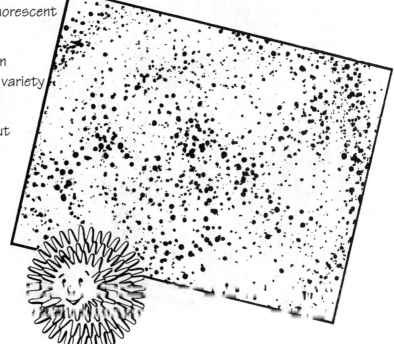

You can also use pinecones, marbles or an assortment of various-sized balls with a variety of textures.

Spiney balls are wonderful for rolling about in play dough and can be used to create textural surfaces in drywall joint compound. (If you are unfamiliar with this art medium, see the Joint Compound section of this book.)

*See supply list on page 136.

DOILY PRINTS

MATERIALS:

Plastic or paper doilies
Sponge brushes
Tempera paint
Containers for paint
Paper or fabric

PROCESS:

Place doily on paper or fabric and use a sponge brush to coat the doily with paint. The more colors, the more interesting the pattern will look as the colors blend and fan out. Lift off doily to see the impression left behind. Add additional doilies or smaller doilies to vary the patterns.

Banners or clothing such as T-shirts can be used. Fabric or acrylic paint will be more permanent. Your doily prints will be wearable and can be laundered. The banners make wonderful gifts.

Hint: The fanning out of colors work best if you sponge brush from the center of the doily to the outer edge.

ROLLERBALL ART

MATERIALS:
Variety of different sized balls
Rubber bands
Circular tubs or containers
   (Bigger balls work best in a small pool.)
Tempera paint
Paper

PROCESS:
Cut paper to fit in the bottom of the tub you've decided to use. Put rubber bands around balls so that they overlap every which way. Dip the balls into paint and place the ball on top of the paper and roll about by grasping the edges of the tub. Use a variety of paint colors and different ball sizes to achieve an interesting pattern.

The patterns created from these rollerballs remind me of chicken prints. It looks as if a chicken got into paint and ran all over the paper.

Try using the really thick rubber bands and use a plastic swimming pool with paper fit into the bottom. Follow the directions above. This procedure allows many children to participate and it's fun!

Idea used with permission by Norbert Siegler.

MAGNET ART

MATERIALS:

Magnetic wands

Magnetic marble ball or other ferro magnetic materials such as paper clips,
nails, gears, etc. (Anything that is small can be used. If it can rust, it's
magnetic metal.)

Cookie sheet (or cookie tin, the round tin pans that are available at
holiday time work great)

Tempera paint

Cup-like containers or pie tins

Spoons

Paper

PROCESS:

Pour paint into cups or pie tins. Cut desired shape paper to fit into cookie tin, cookie sheet or whatever metal surface you'll be using. Have the children pick various magnetic objects and drop into paint. Spoon out the objects and place on cookie sheet. Place the magnetic wand underneath the cookie sheet or tin, and move it around. The objects will dance and move or drag across the paper making painted markings. Replenish the paint on the objects as needed.

Note: If objects are too drenched in paint, they will not move.

Be careful that the materials you use do not present a choking hazard with very young children.

SHOE PRINTS

MATERIALS:
Shoes with interesting patterns on the bottoms
Tempera paint
Paintbrushes
Paper
Containers for paint

PROCESS:
Pour paint into containers. Have the children paint the bottom of the shoes with brushes. Press the painted surface onto the paper to make prints.

Optional Idea: Buy sacks of 16" (40.64 cm) doll accessories that have a variety of shoes. These are fun to make prints of, and the doll shoes fit perfectly on children's fingertips.

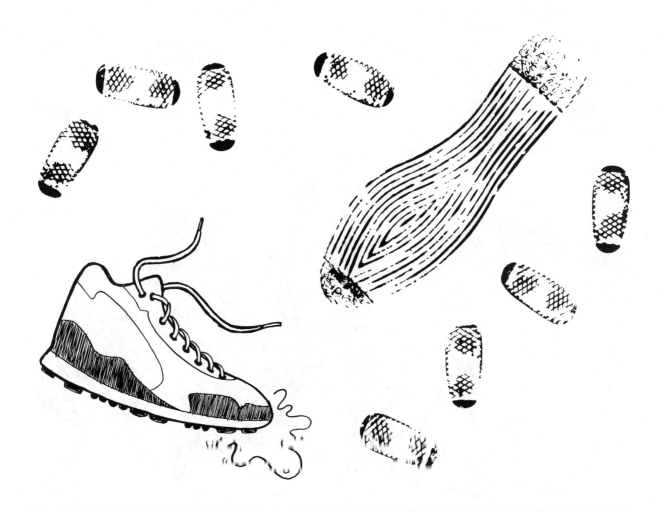

PLEXIGLAS™ PRINTS

MATERIALS:
Various sizes and variety of raised Plexiglas™ designs (can be purchased
    at your local hardware or building supply center)
Tempera paint
Containers for paint
Paintbrushes
Paper

PROCESS:
Pour the paint into containers. Using the paintbrushes, paint the Plexiglas™ design. Try using a variety of different sizes and shapes of brushes to make it more interesting. Place a sheet of paper on top of the painted Plexiglas™ and rub across the back of the paper. The design is transferred onto the paper. You can achieve varying effects with the thickness of paint and by using textured paper. You can also use fabric and make banners or flags.

Pieces of Plexiglas™ are wonderful for imprints with clay and play dough. They make great cover designs if your class is making books. Using black tempera paint on white paper, we made a print and our children painted their hands and placed handprints in random areas.

Don't limit yourself to just one art medium. After your Plexiglas™ print dries, you can collage on it, make it into a place mat or even add a different Plexiglas™ print onto your print with a different color paint. The possibilities are endless. Just take the time to explore and experiment. And always have fun!

PLUG PRINTS

MATERIALS:

Plugs of different sizes from a hardware store (Plugs with a metal ring
     through the top work best and allow children to have something to
     grasp when making their prints.)
Tempera paint
Paper
Shallow containers for paint

PROCESS:

Pour paint into shallow containers, making sure there is enough paint to dip the base of the
plugs, but not so much that the whole plug is covered. Dip the plug into the paint and allow the
excess to drip back into the container. Press plug onto the paper. Scatter plug prints in various
shapes and colors for an interesting effect. If you let the children explore with this art, you will
find them using lots of problem-solving skills.

Optional Idea: Use watered-down bleach in place of paint. Use colored tissue paper and mount
on construction paper or cardboard for heavier backing.

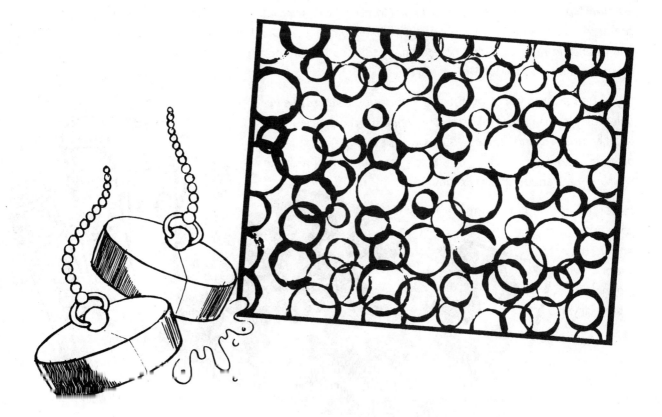

BINGO MARKERS

MATERIALS:

Bingo markers in various colors (These can usually be obtained in
    game section in toy departments or check with bingo suppliers or
    places that play bingo.)
Heavy paper (It does bleed through with thinner paper.)

PROCESS:

Bingo markers are a most wonderful invention! Make sure you purchase bingo markers that are nontoxic if you are working with young children. They come with sponge-tip applicators. Look for the type that the applicator top pops off and can be refilled with watered-down liquid tempera, food coloring or ink. At some bingo suppliers you can even purchase different sponge applicator tops that come in various shapes such as hearts, stars and geometric shapes.

The wonderful thing about this art is that it's fast. You can take it out and set it up in a matter of minutes. It's great for patterning, it's very open-ended and it's fun!

The important thing to remember with the art activity is that the children need to use an up and down motion when using the bingo markers. If they draw or make circular motions, the sponge-tip applicator will rip and the colored ink will drip out. When the up and down motion required to do this activity is explained, it becomes a fun activity with the pounding and thumping noises that indicate the children are very busy being creative!

If you use a large sheet of butcher paper, you can create very colorful gift wrap. The ink from the bingo markers dries quickly, and within minutes you have wrapping paper that you or your child have created. It's much more personal and fun. We rarely purchase gift wrap anymore!

Hint: If you're in a hurry and some of your ink circles aren't drying, hurry them along with a blow dryer!

BATH MAT PRINTS

MATERIALS:

Bath mats with a variety of different suction backings
   (You can cut the mats up to make several squares.)
Paintbrushes
Tempera paint mixed on the thick side
Container for paint
Paper
Optional: Brayers or rolling pins

PROCESS:

Place the bath mats suction cup side facing up, and apply paint. Have the children place a sheet of paper over the top of the just-painted mat, and rub the paper with their hands, transferring the painted pattern onto the paper. Instead of using hands, children can use dry brayers or rolling pins to rub and transfer the painted suction cup patterns onto the paper.

To add variety to this activity, the paper and bath mat can be cut into different shapes.

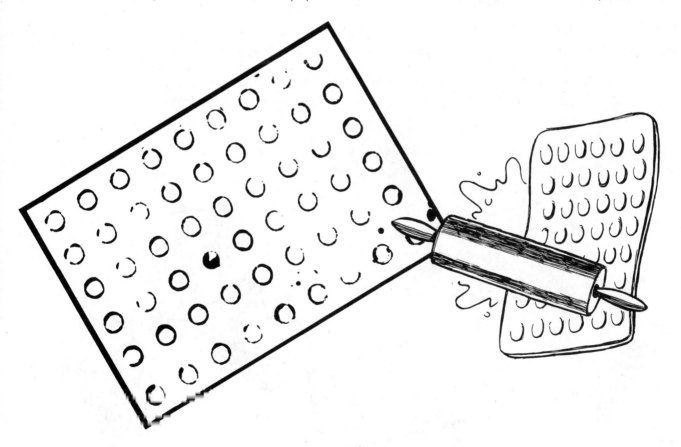

CORK PRINTS

MATERIALS:
Corks of all sizes
Hammer
Small nails
Hot glue gun
Gears and washers
U-shaped nails in corks
Tempera paint
Shallow containers for paint
Brushes
Paper

PROCESS:
Before starting this activity, an adult needs to hammer small nails and U-shaped nails into the bottom of the corks in various patterns. Using a hot glue gun, attach various washers and gears to corks. Now you're ready to begin.

Pour paint into shallow containers. Dip the prepared ends of the corks into paint and press onto paper. Use brushes to smooth out the paint and to brush off excess paint if needed.

Interesting patterns can be created using a variety of materials. Don't limit yourself to just paper. Use colored burlap or fabric squares. Decorate a pillowcase using fabric paint in place of tempera. Create a wall hanging!

Note: Be especially careful when working with small children that the materials you select do not pose a choking hazard or are not so sharp as to cause injury.

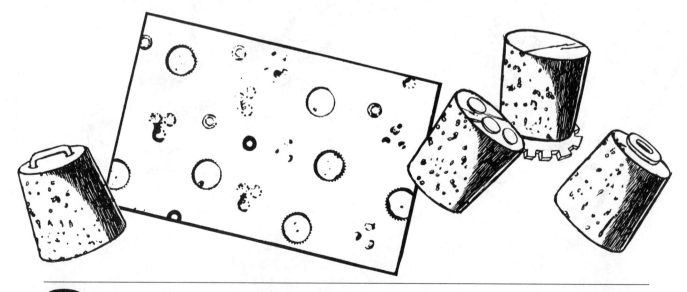

SHAPES ON FILM CANISTERS

MATERIALS:

Small wooden shapes (from craft store or you can cut
    vinyl place mats or foot insoles into desired shapes)
Glue gun
Empty film canisters
Tempera paint
Paintbrushes
Container for paint that wooden shapes fit easily into

PROCESS:

Ahead of time, glue various shapes onto the ends of the film canisters using the hot glue gun.
Which end you use is up to you.

Have children paint the shape and press onto paper for prints.

You can also cut shapes from Styrofoam™ meat trays. These can be "incised" with a pencil or
pen. Patterns, faces and other designs can be added to your shape.

STRAW BUNDLE PRINTS

MATERIALS:

Plastic straws
Rubber bands
Tempera paint
Containers for paint
Paper

PROCESS:

Fill containers with paint. Pie tins work wonderfully. Bundle straws with rubber bands at each end. Vary the bundles making some small and some large. Tap one end of the bundle against a desk or tabletop to even out the surface. Dip an "even" end of a bundle in paint and press down on paper.

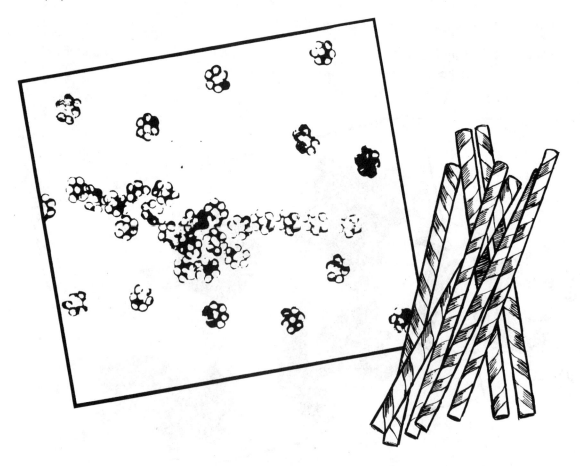

PAPER CLIP PRINTS

MATERIALS:

Paper clips
Spoons, tongs or tweezers
Paper
Tempera paint
Shallow containers for paint

Sometimes when doing art, the results are not too exciting or spectacular. The process is what is important. A lot happens in the process of doing this particular art activity. Paper clips are readily available in most homes and schools, so it is an art activity that's easily set up.

The children use hand and eye coordination to transfer the painted paper clips to the paper with spoons, tongs or tweezers. If you are using various colors of tempera paint, then the child will be color blending (a science activity). They may be clustering groups of clips or creating a pattern (a math experience). By placing the paper on top of the painted paper clips to rub and get a print, the child is following a sequence (logic).

Art needs to be looked upon as a process. It doesn't necessarily have to achieve anything, it's just there to do as you please. As we've stated before, some of the best art never makes it to paper!

PROCESS:

Pour paint into shallow containers. Pie tins as well as meat trays work great for this activity. Children can easily grab a cluster of paper clips from them. Add paper clips to the containers of paint. Using spoons, tongs or tweezers, have the children place the painted clips onto a sheet of paper. The more the better. Then place another sheet of paper on top of the painted paper clips. The child rubs the top paper, being sure to feel all the areas where the clips have been placed. Lift the top paper off and see the impression.

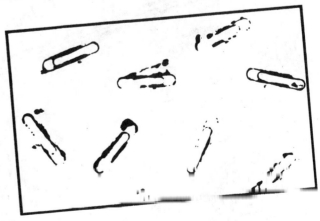

PRINTS AREN'T JUST MADE FROM POTATOES!

YOU CAN MAKE PRINTS FROM:

Feather dusters

Bunion pads on blocks of wood

Berry baskets

Plastic fishing worms

Soap holders (suction cup kind)

Potato mashers (They come in all sizes and shapes.)

Cookie cutters

Fly swatters

Sponges cut into desired shapes

And much, much more!

ALL YOU NEED IS
PAPER,
PAINT
AND A LITTLE IMAGINATION!

HAVE FUN!

GLOVE PRINTS

MATERIALS:
Package of latex gloves (surgical type)
Bunion pads, corn pads
Tempera paint
Brushes
Paper

PROCESS:
Put on the glove and stick on various bunion pads and corn pads creating whatever pattern you'd like. Take a brush and paint the glove while your hand is inside. Press your hand or hands across the paper making prints and patterns. It's a wonderful, oozy feeling!

After completion of your picture, take your gloved hand to the sink or water tub and wash off. It can then be hung up for another child to use. Make, or have the children make, many patterned gloves.

We do a lot of hand painting in our class, and the children love the feel. But with this variation, you can feel the cool paint and its texture, but your hands stay clean inside the glove!

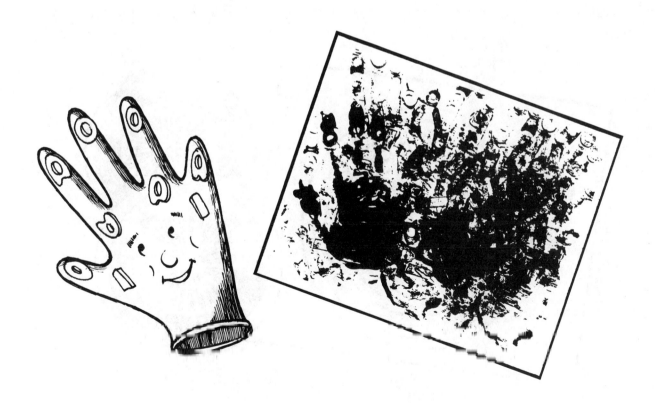

SPIDERWEB PRINTS

MATERIALS:

Plastic plate holders (These can be purchased in the picnic section of
  department stores.)
Tempera paint (You can use any color.)
Brushes or prepsicles*
Paper

PROCESS:

Turn the paper plate holder over. Some holders have very interesting patterns on the back. They make wonderful prints. Don't limit yourself to just spiderwebs.

Brush on the paint. Sponge brushes work the best. After painting the back of the plate holder, place a piece of paper over the top and rub, transferring the painted pattern to the paper.

Another option is to brush watered-down glue onto the paper plate holder and place a sheet of paper on top and rub. Then sprinkle glitter, shaking off the excess.

Optional Idea: You can make spiders to put on your webs. We make ours from construction paper scraps, a figure eight shape approximately the size of a quarter. We make the legs from strips of the same construction paper, folding them accordion style. (Spiders have eight legs.) The kids love using paper reinforcements for eyes so they have the appearance of google-eyed spiders.

*See supply list on page 136.

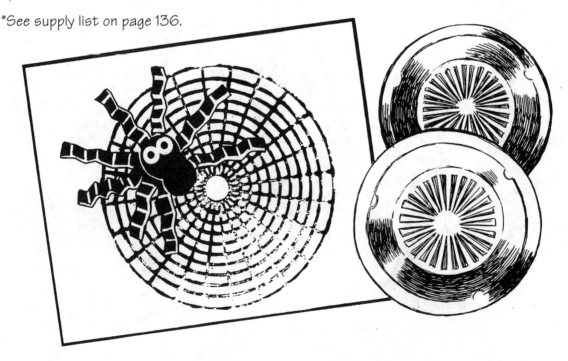

BATTING ART

MATERIALS:
Batting
Tempera paint
Brushes
Pie tins
Paper

PROCESS:
Mix paint in pie tins. Have three or four colors to choose from. Give each child some batting to paint on. You can give them large sheets of batting or a small sheet. Let the children paint the batting. When they are done painting, let them lay a sheet of paper on top of the batting, rub the paper and pull the paper off. The print they get from the rubbing is neat!

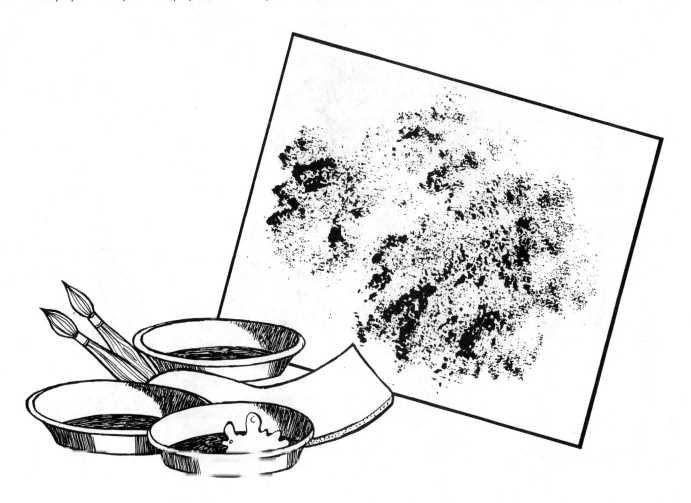

LOOFAH PRINTS

MATERIALS:
Loofahs (These come in fine, medium and coarse.)
Tempera paint
Paper
Pie tins

PROCESS:
Loofahs make great prints for sponge paints and are very easy to use with children of all ages. Since loofah sponges can be costly, I ask parents to buy the sponges and contribute them to the class. They are usually more than happy to do so.

When you get your loofahs, offer a variety of paint colors in pie tins. Let the children explore with many different colors. Put loofahs into the pie tins, and let the children paint with them. Offer several varieties of loofahs to make the art experience more exciting.

HORSE TACK PRINTS

MATERIALS:
Horse brushes of various kinds (can be found at feed and tack stores)
Paper
Tempera paint
Pie tins

PROCESS:
My hobby is riding horses. One day while I was brushing my horse, I thought what a great print the horse brush would make on paper. I then went to my tack barn and started finding all kinds of horse equipment that would be great to use with the children in my preschool in an art activity.

Mix various colors of tempera paint in pie tins and put horse brushes into each of the pie tins. Let the children paint with the brushes on their paper. There is no right or wrong way to paint with the brushes. Let them explore! Some horse brushes make really interesting prints.

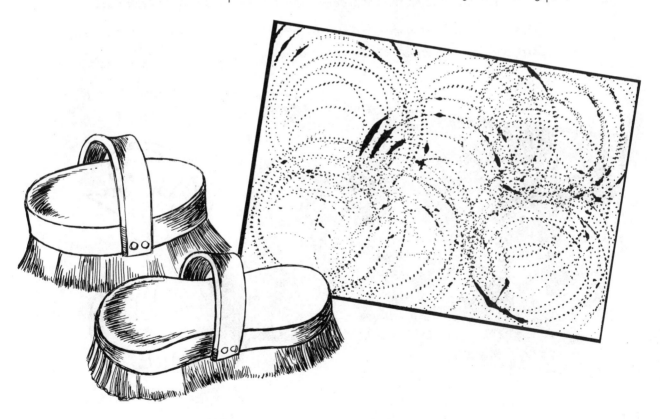

BUNDLE PRINTS

MATERIALS:

Some suggested items to be used for making your bundles: package bubbles, a paper towel, plastic wrap with holes in it, jar gripper, mesh bag that fruits come in, burlap, scraps of material, etc.

Filler: cotton balls (You can use old rags, polyester filling, etc.)

Yarn, rubber bands or twist ties (what you will be using to tie off your bundles)

Tempera paint

Shallow containers for paint

Paper

PROCESS:

To make your bundle, cut a small square of the item you will be using. Interesting textural surfaces make the best prints. Take a cotton ball or whatever you will be using for a filler, and put it in the middle of your square. Bring up the sides and tie securely so that you have a small bundle. Make up several using many different items. Now you are ready to make prints!

Dip the bundle into the shallow container of paint and press down onto paper. Use a variety of textures and colors, and see all the patterns you can create.

Have fun!

BALLOON PRINTS

MATERIALS:
Small balloons
Paper
Tempera paint
Pie tins

PROCESS:
Mix up as many different colors of paint as you would like the children to explore. Pie tins work well for mixing paint, as do meat trays. Blow up balloons and tie them off, keeping in mind that little hands will be grabbing these balloons. Don't blow them up too big. Take the balloons that you have blown up, and put them into the pie tins with the different colors of paint. The children can now paint by pressing up and down with the balloons. They make wonderful prints!

MAKING YOUR OWN TILE BASE

This idea came from Bev Bos. It is very open-ended art and allows children to be creative. By making your own, you or a child can create a personal tile base that can be used over and over again. At the cooperative preschool where Bev teaches, they have used an outside wall on one of the buildings and adhered the tiles to it. The kids can paint the tiles and make prints. What a great idea!

Your tile base can be made on a small square or rectangle for an individual to paint on or a longer rectangle for several children to work on together.

MATERIALS:

Ceramic tiles from wallpaper stores or building supply stores (Many places will sell you discontinued stock very economically, and wallpaper stores may give you old tile samples free. Don't forget that garage sales are a great source for some really good stuff!)

Tube of silicone caulking (This is the stuff that you use in your bathroom around your tub.)

Masonite cut in the length or shape desired (We usually use ¼" to ½" [.6 to 1.25 cm] thick.)

PROCESS:

On the back of the tiles, squirt out the silicone caulking and mount the tiles onto the masonite base. Because you will want this to be waterproof for cleanup, make sure the back of the tiles as well as the masonite below the tiles are covered generously. Let it set up for twenty-four hours before using.

Idea used with permission by Bev Bos.

PAINTING ON TILES

MATERIALS:
Tile base (page 24)
Tempera paint
Brushes
Paper
Bowl of soapy water and rag

PROCESS:
Paint the tiles using the tempera paint. After desired design is completed, take a sheet of paper and place on top of the wet paint, rubbing it to pick up the entire pattern. After the print has been transferred to paper, take the bowl of soapy water and the rag, and clean up the tile base so that it is ready for the next artist!

PACKAGE BUBBLE PRINTS

MATERIALS:

Package bubbles (This is a great way to recycle some that you've received, or you can get these at package mailing places, moving stores that carry boxes and trailers, and the post office.) I like to get assorted sizes. The big bubbles are really fun, but try to resist popping all of them as they don't print once the bubble has been popped!

Large sheet of newsprint or butcher paper

Tempera paint

Paintbrushes

Containers for paints

Masking tape

Bowl of soapy water and a washcloth or rag

PROCESS:

Cut a large piece of package bubbles and tape down with masking tape. Be sure the bubbles are bubble side up. We usually put wads of masking tape underneath the bubbles to make sure it is secured and will not move when painted. Put out tempera paints with the brushes. Paint the bubbles. Lay a piece of paper on the top and rub, making a print from the painted design. Clean with washcloth and soapy water, and it is ready for the next child. Children love doing this step! It's not necessary to clean the crevices between each bubble because the paper only picks up the print from the raised bubbles.

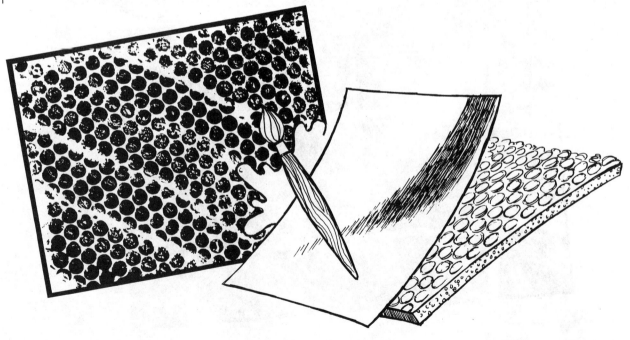

"TOTALLY TUBULAR" ART

MATERIALS:

Toilet paper tubes, paper towel tubes
Masking tape
Roll of packaging bubbles
Bunion pads, corn pads
Weather stripping (self-adhesive kind sold in hardware stores)
Scissors
Large sheet of paper (newsprint or butcher paper)
Tempera paint
Containers long and shallow enough to put paint into and roll tubes around or
    containers to put paint into using brushes to paint the tubes
Cellophane tape or glue to mount the bubbles to the tube

PROCESS:

Wrap the packaging bubbles (bubble side out) around the paper towel tube. You can adhere it to the tube by taping it with cellophane tape, glue or even use a glue gun. Take two toilet paper rolls and squeeze each roll into the paper towel roll on each side. Now you have handles that make it easier to roll. Tape them securely with the masking tape. On another paper towel roll you can adhere the weather stripping to make a pattern. On still another paper towel roll, place bunion pads and corn pads. Now you're ready to paint!

Dip the roller into the paint and roll across the paper. If you do not have a container long enough to put paint into and roll about freely, then just have the children use paintbrushes to paint the tubes and then roll.

Don't worry about trying to clean the tubes after the art is done. Just let them eventually wear out and then throw them away. The paint will dry and when you take them out to use another day, you will be putting on fresh paint. You could wipe off the package bubble tube if you like, with a rag or sponge. What a great recycling art activity—and fun!

Idea used with permission by Jeanette Anchondo.

TEMPERA BUBBLE PRINTS

MATERIALS:

Pie tins or containers that are shallow but deep enough to place cookie
 cutters into wet paint
Assortment of plastic cookie cutters
Tempera paint
Paper
Dawn® dishwashing detergent

PROCESS:

Mix Dawn® dishwashing detergent and paint into a pie tin. You will need a generous portion of soap in order to produce a bubble. Mix several paints with soaps to have a variety of colors. Place cookie cutter into the pie tin of soap and paint. Carefully pick up the cookie cutter, forming a bubble within the shape. Place the cookie cutter onto the paper, and the swirled bubble shape will pop leaving a painted impression!

COMB PRINTS

MATERIALS:

Combs of various sizes
Tempera paint
Butcher paper
Towel and container of water

PROCESS:

Mix three to four different colors of tempera in paint containers. Give each child two pieces of butcher paper. Have them lay the combs down on one sheet of the paper. Make sure you have lots of different sizes of combs for the children to use. When they have finished laying their combs on the paper, they are ready to paint the combs. If the combs start to slide around while the children are painting them, try taping them to the paper. When the children are done painting the combs, have them lay the other sheet of paper on top of the painted combs and rub. When they are done rubbing all the combs they have painted, peel the paper off, and they will have a print.

Have the children take the combs they just painted and put them in a container of water to wash and dry them so the combs are ready for the next child. We have noticed that some children like washing and drying the combs more than they do painting them. That's okay. The process is more important than the finished product.

BAND-AID™ ART PICTURES

This art activity came about from a desire to fulfill a preschooler's dream—unwrapping Band-Aids™! I have found it fascinating that children, regardless of age, seem to know how to unwrap a Band-Aid™! There are such wonderfully colorful Band-Aids™ and such interesting sizes and widths that this activity can pose a geometric challenge in art!

Because Band-Aids™ can be costly, have each child bring a box or start a donation box prior to Band-Aid™ Art Day!

MATERIALS:

Assortment of Band-Aids™ in various sizes, widths and colors
Cardboard or tagboard
Tempera paint
Brayers or small roller (Paint rollers are available in hardware stores.)
Shallow containers for paint (Meat containers work great! Make sure brayer or roller fits into it easily.)
Paper (type and texture is whatever is readily available to you)
Paintbrushes

PROCESS:

Have the children open and peel back the portion of the Band-Aid™ that will stick to the cardboard. Invite the children to stick the Band-Aids™ onto the cardboard in any pattern that pleases them. After creating their pictures or patterns, they can now make a print. Have several tempera paint colors available, or go with a negative/positive look with black and white tempera paint. Pour the paint into shallow containers. Let the children dip the brayers into the paint and roll the color onto their Band-Aid™ pictures. They may want to use paintbrushes to cover some areas. Now place a sheet of paper over the top of the Band-Aid™ picture and rub or use a rolling pin or unpainted brayer over the surface of the paper to pick up the texture. Try to pick up the various outlines and small holes in the Band-Aids™ as well as all the paint. Pull the paper off and you have a Band-Aid™ picture print as well as a cardboard Band-Aid™ picture! The cardboard picture can be used to make several pictures, to transfer to various areas on a large sheet of butcher paper to make a larger design or to make your own wrapping paper!

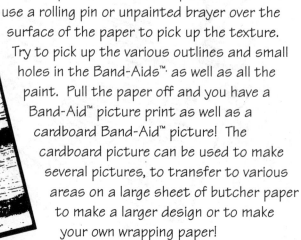

CORRUGATED PAPER ART

MATERIALS:

Tempera paint
Corrugated paper
Paintbrushes
Paper
Pie tins

PROCESS:

You can buy corrugated paper through most educational catalogs. It comes in packs of twelve sheets. You can also buy it in rolls of 48" x 5' (1.22 x 1.52 m) as well as 48" x 25' (1.22 x 7.62 m). If you want to have the children paint a mural, the bigger rolls are great. We like using the larger rolls because it encourages children to work together, which enhances creativity and gives children a rich environment for the development of fine motor skills and problem-solving skills.

Mix up some tempera paint, give the children paintbrushes and let them start painting on the corrugated paper. You can also give them smaller sheets of the corrugated paper to paint. When they are done painting, give them a sheet of butcher paper to lay over the painted corrugated paper. Have them rub the paper and pull it back. What they get is a really neat print of what they just painted.

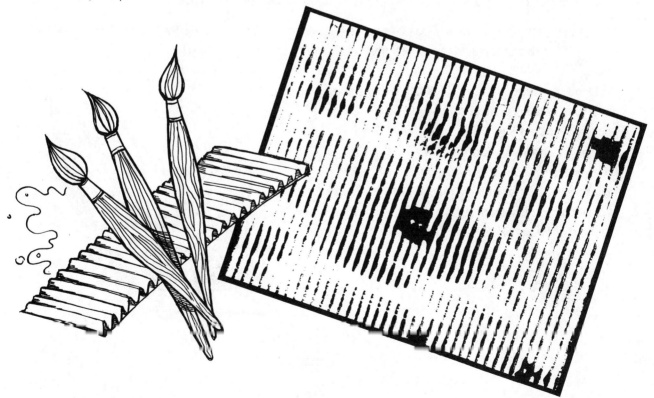

CORNCOB ART

MATERIALS:
Tempera paint
Pie tins
Corncobs
Paper

PROCESS:
Because art is such an important part of our program and we explore so many different ways of doing art, the children have a tendency to get excited about trying some of their own ideas. That is how we came upon corncob art. One of the children in our program came to preschool with corncobs and wanted to know if he could paint them to see what kind of print they would make. Being the creative teachers that we are, we thought it was important to honor his request.

In pie tins we mixed up four colors of paint—his choice of course. Then we put corncobs into each pie tin. The children then took large sheets of paper, long enough to roll the corncobs across, and started painting with them.

I must say that the process is much more important than the finished product. We discovered that the prints from the corncobs weren't all that great, but the kids had a blast!

When confronted with "crazy" art ideas, ask yourself what the children will gain from doing the art. Here are some questions I ask myself when I come up with a wild idea:
1) Does it promote creativity? 2) Is exploring a variety of art media enjoyable? 3) What will the children get out of this art developmentally? Does it develop hand-eye coordination as well as large and small muscle control? 4) Does it make them feel good about themselves? My answer to all these questions, when confronted with the corncob art idea was "Yes!"

DRYER LINT ART

MATERIALS:

Dryer lint
Poster board
Adhesive spray
Collage materials such as embroidery thread, glitter, confetti, etc.

PROCESS:

Let lint accumulate in the lint catcher of your dryer. Peel it off of the screen and save it until you have collected enough for this activity. Dryer lint is great for collaging. Before you let the children collage with the dryer lint, you will need to spray a small piece of cardboard or poster board with adhesive spray. Lay dryer lint on all areas of the adhesive poster board. After positioning the dryer lint, spray adhesive onto the lint. The children can now collage directly onto the dryer lint. Allow a day for the picture to fully dry. You can cover the dryer lint collage with clear adhesive paper if you don't want to wait for the artwork to dry.

Note: Be sure to spray adhesive in a well-ventilated area or outside. When working with young children, you may want to have the dryer lint already mounted. You may also want to spray the lint so the children can just concentrate on collaging.

RUBBER BAND STAMPS

MATERIALS:
Wood blocks
Rubber bands
Ink pad
Double-sided carpet tape

PROCESS:
There are many ways to create rubber stamps, but using rubber bands is one of the simplest ways to make stamps with young children that is truly open-ended. The best kind of rubber bands to use are the really thick ones. Buy lots of them and have fun!

Place carpet tape onto a "stamping-size" block. Cut rubber bands in half and place onto the block. The rubber bands will stick to the carpet tape. You can make shapes, flowers and various abstract designs.

Press the rubber band stamp onto an ink pad and make as many stamped designs as you like!

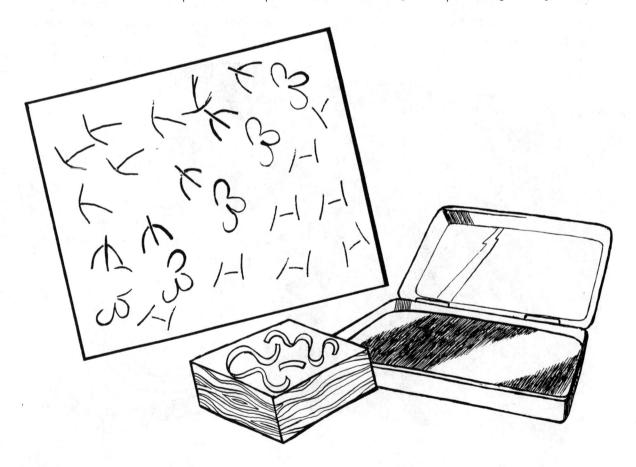

FURNACE FILTER ORNAMENTS

MATERIALS:

Metal portion of furnace filters

Clear adhesive paper

Collage items that will fit into circle openings of the filter, such as dried flowers,
    small pictures (make or cut from old cards or gift wrap), pretty threads or
    string, confetti, metallic sequins or circles, etc.

Wire or metal cutters to cut desired shape from filter

PROCESS:

Cut a piece of the adhesive paper to fit the back of the shape you have cut from the filter. Fill
the circles with collage items. Place another piece of adhesive paper over the top of the filter
thus sealing the collage items inside and sandwiching the filter between the two sheets. Put a
small hole at the top of your ornament, and put a string though the hole so it can be hung as an
ornament or sun catcher.

Idea used with permission by Karen Stafford.

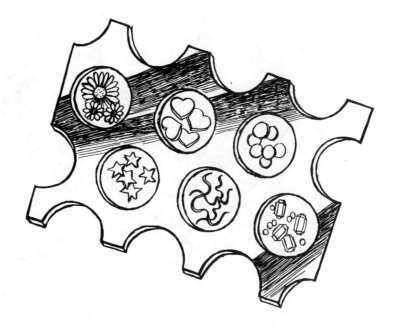

SHADOW BOXES

MATERIALS:
TV dinner trays or lunch trays that have many small compartments
Collage materials
Glue or clear adhesive paper

PROCESS:
You can let the children arrange the collage materials in the compartments of the tray. When the children are satisfied with their design, let them glue the materials directly onto the tray.

Or you can cut out various shapes through the back of tray with a razor or scissors. Cut out pieces of clear adhesive paper to adhere comfortably to the back. Add various collage items to personalize your own shadow box. The items will stick and light will shine through the open spaces of clear adhesive paper. If desired, you can cover the outside with clear wrap and glue-gun ribbon or yarn around the outside edge and add a string hanger from the top.

Note: With younger children, it is easier to have the holes in the back already cut and the clear adhesive paper in place so they can just collage the items in their compartments.

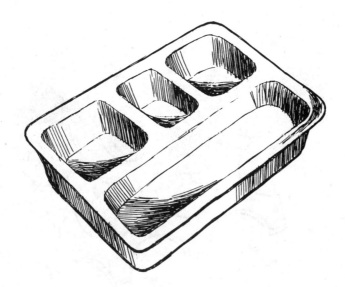

RIBBON BALLS

MATERIALS:

Self-moisten ribbons
Bag of round balloons
Scissors
Optional: Glitter or diamond dust, glue for adding glitter

PROCESS:

Blow balloon up to tennis ball size. It is important that you don't inflate the balloon much larger than this. The smaller size is necessary for this activity to be truly successful with young children. Cut ribbon various lengths so it can be placed over and around the balloon. Moisten the ribbon with water and stick it around the balloon so the ends overlap one another. Wrap ribbon in various patterns. Make sure each end overlaps the other. Use more than one color for a colorful effect. Glitter can be added for that extra sparkle. Allow to dry and pop the balloon and remove. Add a bow if you'd like and some string to hang it up! Keep in mind that it is the process that is important, not the finished product. The children really like to moisten the ribbon, and they will want to make these balls over and over again. Make sure you have plenty of ribbon on hand!

TILE TRIVETS OR MAGNETS

MATERIALS:
Light-colored ceramic tiles (trivet size)
Permanent markers in lots of colors
Magnetic strip with adhesive back
Acrylic gloss medium and varnish (water soluble—available in craft stores)
Felt

TRIVET PROCESS:
Draw a picture on the tile. Brush on gloss medium with brush strokes going in the same direction. Place in low oven (100°F [37.7°C] —or WARM setting) and leave for three to five minutes. If left too long, the gloss turns brown and burns. Watch carefully and put the tile in the oven just long enough to dry the gloss medium. Cool. Glue felt to the back of the trivet so it will not scratch surfaces. Two or three applications of gloss medium puts a stronger protective coat on the trivet.

MAGNET PROCESS:
Using small light-colored tiles, draw a picture design with permanent markers. Brush on an even coating of acrylic gloss medium. Let it air dry or bake in low oven. Cool. Cut a magnetic strip and adhere to the back. Your magnet is ready to place on a refrigerator or file cabinet!

JUICE LID MOBILE

MATERIALS:

Juice lids (Three is a good number for each mobile, but do use more if you want to
    play with balance. I will use three for these directions.)
Small hammer
Nails
Permanent markers
Fish line
Scissors for cutting the fish line
Tongue depressors

PROCESS:

Have the children draw pictures or designs on the juice lids with permanent markers. Then take
a nail and pound a pattern of indentations into the lid. Be sure to have a board or something
underneath that can take the impact of hammering and not damage your working surface. If
your children hammer lightly, they will create a relief design. If they hammer harder, they will
pierce through the lid, allowing light to shine through.

At the top of each lid, hammer one hole that will be used for stringing. Using a nail, make three
holes in the tongue depressor, one on each end and one in the middle.

Cut a desired length from the fish line and tie one end on
the juice lid and the other through the hole in the
tongue depressor. Knot the fish line so it doesn't
come out. The middle juice lid line is longer,
and I allow an additional fish line loop with
some line attached to the top that can be
used for hanging. String the remaining lid.
Make sure the lids can bump into one
another slightly as they make a wonderful
sound!

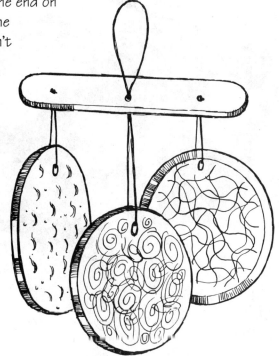

COLORED GLUE MONOPRINTS

MATERIALS:

Mix desired amount of glue with two or three drops of food coloring and pour into
   bottles that will allow you to squirt and drizzle out.
Poster board, tagboard or cardboard cut into various shapes
Construction paper or additional poster board shapes

PROCESS:

Have the children create various abstract designs on a piece of poster board or cardboard with
the glue. Next have the child transfer the design to another paper or piece of poster board. By
turning and twisting the original print, an interesting monoprint is transferred with raised and
swirled effects. The design can be transferred several times and placed differently each time,
depending on how big the paper or poster board is that the child is transferring onto. Children
enjoy the swirled effects created by twisting the glue.

PLASTIC WRAP RELIEF ART

MATERIALS:
Roll of plastic wrap
Glue
Spoon or squirt bottle
Tempera paint
Construction paper or butcher paper cut in abstract shapes

PROCESS:
Mix a few drops of glue into tempera paint. Have the children either spoon or squirt the paint onto the paper. Add plastic wrap to the painting by placing it on top. Make sure the sheet of plastic wrap is oversized to allow plenty of room to scrunch and gather the wrap to create an abstract relief design. If too much paint is concentrated in one area and is not drying, you may poke a tiny hole in the wrap in that area to allow for better ventilation. (Use a needle or straight pin.) After drying (it could take several days), the edges of plastic wrap can be cut off or just folded over to the back of the paper.

OIL AND WATER ART

MATERIALS:
Cake pan
Water
Oil-based enamel paint
Paper
Craft sticks

PROCESS:
Partly fill a shallow cake pan with water. Dribble several colors of oil-based enamel paint across the water. Swirl the puddles of paint with a craft stick. Lay a sheet of paper on the surface of the water. Tap it gently, then lift it off and lay it down flat to dry. It could take a whole day to dry.

Optional Idea: Cut various shapes out of a heavy tagboard or poster board. Ornaments to hang in the window, on a door, on a tree or on a necklace can be made and strung on ribbon or yarn.

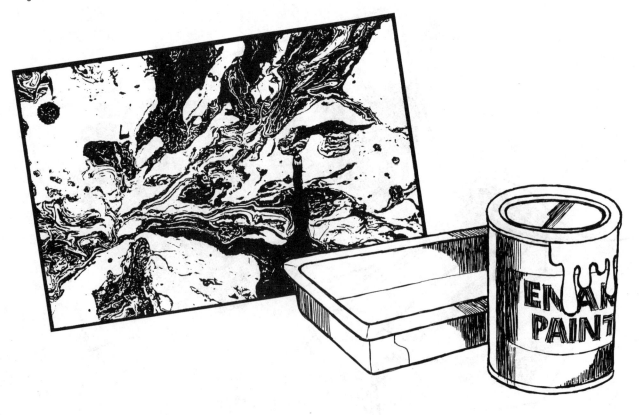

MAKE YOUR OWN STICKERS

MATERIALS:
Wrapping paper scraps
Drawings or magazine pictures
Brush to apply glue

Recipe for Sticker Glue
8 T (120 ml) vinegar
4 packets of unflavored gelatin
1 T (15 ml) peppermint extract

In a small saucepan, bring vinegar to a boil. Add the unflavored gelatin, reduce to low heat and stir until gelatin is completely dissolved. Add peppermint extract and mix it well. Cool. Makes about ½ cup (125 ml).

PROCESS:
Brush glue on back of wrapping paper sheet or drawing. Use sparingly. Let dry. Paper may curl but will straighten when the sticker is applied.

If glue should harden while brushing on, place in a large pan of hot water and let glue soften. Save leftover glue in a tightly capped bottle. It will keep for several months.

To soften glue after storage, a warming tray dissolves the glue nicely. Warm about an hour before use.

Moisten the paper to activate glue and apply as stickers.

PAINT WITH CORN SYRUP

MATERIALS:

Corn syrup
Food coloring
Containers
Brushes
Paper or white paper plates

PROCESS:

Mix a small amount of corn syrup with desired food coloring. Pour into containers. (Paper cups work great.) Using brushes, paint onto paper or paper plates. It takes several days to dry, and it's sticky to touch even after drying. The colors are spectacular, and it's a great art activity to demonstrate the texture "sticky."

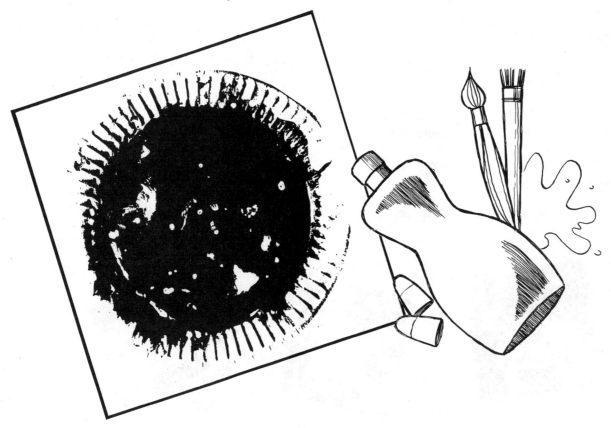

POTTERY WHEEL ART

MATERIALS:
Pottery wheel
T-shirt or material
Acrylic paints or fabric paints
Pushpins
Squirt bottle with water

PROCESS:
Mount T-shirt to pottery wheel with pushpins. Spin pottery wheel. Drizzle paints on shirt or material as wheel spins. Stop wheel. If desired, spray with water in areas that you want the paint to spread or fan out. Spin the wheel again. Unpin item and hang to dry.

Note: Wash as usual. Paint does not run or wash out. On fabric paints, follow the directions listed on the product.

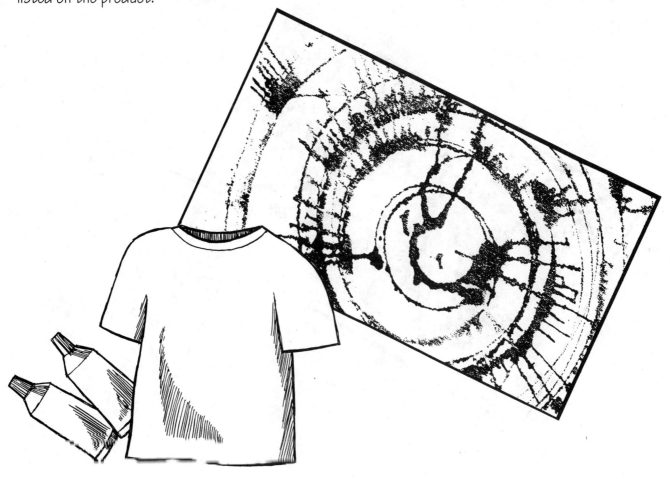

CON-TACT™ COLLAGE

MATERIALS:
Adhesive paper
Collage items
Glue stick
Construction paper or poster board

PROCESS:
Cut adhesive paper into desired shape. Glue-stick the nonsticky side to construction paper or poster board for support. Peel backing paper off to expose sticky side. Sprinkle collage items on sticky side.

Optional Idea: Colorful plastic ends from cable wires make wonderful collage relief pictures. Any circuit board assembly plant or telephone company can be contacted to save their cable wire ends.

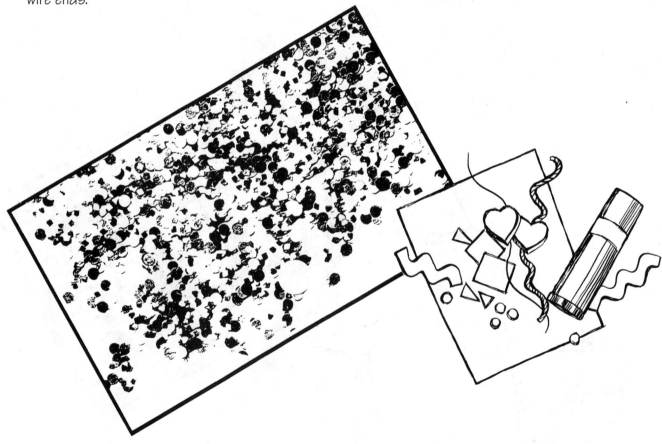

DRIED GLUE PAINTINGS

MATERIALS:

All-purpose glue, full strength
Cardboard or tagboard
Combs, nails, craft sticks, pencils, forks or other blunt items that will make
  trail patterns in the glue
Assortment of tempera paint
Containers for paint
Brushes

PROCESS:

This is a two-day process unless the weather is sunny, and you can begin the process in the morning and complete the next step in the afternoon.

Pour a generous amount of glue onto a piece of tagboard or cardboard. Let the child draw into the glue with combs, nails, craft sticks, pencils with pointy tips, forks and other items that will make grooves and trail patterns. Set aside to dry.

When the glue is dry, it will be clear. This is a fun process for children as they can see the white glue as they draw their patterns and designs. When it is dry, it appears to be gone! Then they can paint the cardboard and their patterns and designs appear again!

IVORY SNOW™ PAINTINGS

MATERIALS:

One box of Ivory Snow™ detergent
Water
Bowl for mixing
Manual hand beaters
Containers for detergent (margarine tubs work well)
Craft sticks or plastic spoons for stirring colors
Brushes
Food coloring or tempera paint
Construction paper, butcher paper or other paper that can take the moisture
   Cardboard works great, too!

PROCESS:

Combine 1 cup (250 ml) of water with 3 cups (750 ml) of Ivory Snow™ detergent. Use the manual hand beaters and mix until creamy and thick. This will make enough mixture for a dozen kids to paint with depending on the size of your paper. The kids love helping with the beaters. It's a great dexterity experience! You can spoon the soap mixture into containers, add a drop or two of food coloring and mix each container well. Liquid tempera paint can also be added if food coloring is not available. Tempera paint will have a granular look in the mixture. Dip the brushes into the mixture and paint. When dry, the mixture has a textured surface. Wash your brushes out with warm water after completion of art. Pull combs through your painting while it is wet for a different effect.

Another option is to use flat pie tins or meat trays to spoon the soap mixture into when adding color. Take cookie cutters or gadgets, dip them in the detergent mixture and press onto the paper. Glitter can be added when wet if desired. These make wonderful cards for various holidays!

Still another variation is to use black paper and not color the Ivory Snow™. It makes wonderful winter scenes, and the black and white contrast really stands out!

CRAYON MELTS

Crayon-melt art has been around forever! We remember doing this favorite art activity when we were kids. Now that we are teachers, it is one of our favorite mediums to use with kids. On a rainy or snowy day, put the materials out on the table, and you will have a group of children around the table all day long!

MATERIALS:
Crayons (fat crayons work very well)
Warming tray (Try to find one in a second-hand store.)
Tagboard
Roll of paper towels

PROCESS:
Cover your table with newspaper. Plug in the warming tray, and let it warm up before you let the children begin this activity. Make sure you have lots and lots of crayons for the children to use. The fat crayons are best because they're easy for young children to hold, and they do not melt as fast. Don't use crayons that are too short, or the children's fingers will come too close to the surface of the warming tray. Once the children melt the colors they want onto the warming tray, give them a strip of tagboard and have them press the tagboard firmly down on the melted crayon and lift up and press down again. Children can continue doing this until they get their strips of tagboard covered with melted crayon. As each child finishes, have him wipe the warming tray with paper towels, and then you are ready for the next child to explore with this art medium.

Try covering the warming tray with foil, and let the children melt their crayons on the foil. When each child is done, have her remove the foil from the warming tray. The foil is their artwork. The next child can then cover the warming tray with a clean sheet of foil. What I like about using foil is that is so different from paper, and the children like using it as well. You can also use scrap paper, butcher paper, tissue paper, etc. Metallic crayons are also fun! Explore!

Idea used with permission by Kristin Parker, a preschool teacher.

SANDPAPER ART

MATERIALS:

Iron
Small table-size ironing board
Crayons
Sandpaper

PROCESS:

Color a picture or design on the sandpaper. Lay design on the paper, crayon side down, and iron the back of the sandpaper using a low to medium setting. The picture or design transfers onto the paper with an interesting effect.

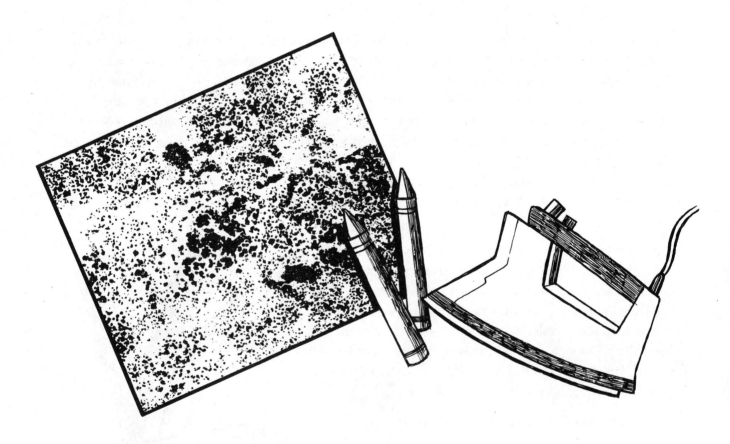

DREAM CATCHER

MATERIALS:

Embroidery hoops
Permanent markers
String or yarn
Beads (size: small)
Feathers

PROCESS:

Let the children color the embroidery hoop with the marker. Take off the outer hoop leaving the inner hoop for the children to wrap the string around. You may want a parent helper to assist with this project. Have the parent helper hold the hoop as the child wraps the string around the hoop. Have the child loop the string around the hoop three times then stop and string on a bead. Loop string around three more times and string on another bead. Finish looping the string around the whole hoop making sure to leave some string hanging at the bottom of the hoop for three beads and a feather. You are now ready to put the outer hoop back around the inner hoop. To finish, let the children string three beads and the feather. You may want to use a glue gun to keep the beads and feather from falling off. Put string on top of the hoop, and let the children take it home.

We did a theme on nighttime fears and explored ways we could overcome those fears. A lot of children in class were having problems with bad dreams, and they were unable to sleep by themselves. I wanted to come up with a project that would help them work through their fear. At the same time I received a gift of a dream catcher from my brother-in-law. After working out a way to make this project as child-direct as possible, the children made and took home their dream catchers. The next day the children were excited about how their dream catchers had taken away their bad dreams. I'll never forget the looks of wonder and the feelings of power that it gave them to know they had made something that could take away those feelings of fear. What power for a child!

DREAM CATCHER (cont'd.)

The Legend of the Dream Catcher

The web of the dream catcher filters all dreams. Good dreams pass through the center hole down the feather to the sleeping person. The bad dreams are trapped in the web where they perish in the light of dawn.

Dream catchers were hung in a lodge or teepee, and also on a baby's cradle board. The dream catcher was kept throughout life and its power enhanced with fetishes and personal belongings.

It is believed the dream catcher originated with the Oneida Indians from northeastern woodlands. The Ojibway and Lakota along with other Native Americans adopted its legend.

A book you might want to read to your children about dream catchers is *Dreamcatcher* by Audrey Osofsky. Illustrated by Ed Young, New York: Orchard Books, 1992.

MARBLING WITH STARCH

This is an affordable process to do with children. The results are spectacular! (Other forms of marbling use carrageenan and can be far too costly to do with a group of children.) You may want to explore the process further by going to your library and reading up on ancient paper decorating.

Marbling is so called because the waves and veined patterns are often like true marble. The patterns you can create are limitless. Marbling results from the designs and patterns that float on a surface of liquid. Many of you have probably taken a container of water and floated oil-base paints on the surface and then used a comb, craft stick or knitting needle to slowly drag through the paint to create a pattern. Oil and water do not mix, so the pattern floats on the surface of the water until you put a piece of paper on the pattern, tap it gently and transfer the pattern to your paper. This same process will occur when we marble with starch.

MATERIALS:

Jug of starch, full strength
Two plastic tubs
Container of water for pouring or access to a sink with a faucet
Items to drag through paint such as picks, combs, knitting needles, small whisk
Acrylic paints
Distilled water
Eyedroppers or pipettes*
Small paper cups
Construction paper or drawing paper that can withstand having
    water poured over it

*See supply list on page 136.

PROCESS:

Put together a variety of acrylic colors that compliment each other. (I would choose at least four.) Take a dab of paint and mix the distilled water with the pipettes or eyedropper. You do not want the paint too watery or too thick. It should be able to go up into the dropper easily and squirt out easily.

MARBLING WITH STARCH *(cont'd.)*

Take your plastic tub (it needs to be bigger than your paper), and fill it with about a half bottle of full-strength starch. Now squirt colors randomly onto the starch. Gently take the tools you will use to drag and create your pattern moving slowly through the paint. Jerking motions will cause the pattern to be lost or the colors smeared into goo. As you slowly drag through the paint, you will actually see the object you are using, pulling and making a pattern. You can create waves, feathering and flowered bursts of color.

Lay your paper onto the pattern of paint and gently tap it. Pick up your paper carefully and wash off the starch. If you do not have access to running water, lay your picture in a clean plastic tub and pour water on top of your pattern, washing the starch away. Your pattern is already absorbed into the paper. You now have a spectacular marbled piece of paper. Some suggestions for use are wrapping paper, bookmarkers, covers for books you are making and greeting cards.

RECORD PLAYER ART

MATERIALS:
Paper plates
Duct tape
Markers
Child's phonograph (Make sure the turntable works.)

PROCESS:
Put duct tape on the turntable making sure that the sticky side of the duct tape is up so the paper plate will stick to the turntable. Now place the paper plate on the turntable. Plug in the phonograph, turn it on and let the children take a marker and hold it down on the plate. The marker will start drawing. Make sure the children don't press down so hard on the turntable that it stops moving. The children will do this art forever, so make sure you have lots of paper plates!

Optional Idea: The watercolors from Germany are another great art medium to use with the phonograph. They are spectacular! You can order the watercolors from Discount School Supply. See the supply list on page 136 for more information.

CANNED MILK RELIEF PICTURES

MATERIALS:
Canned milk (room temperature)
Glass cake pan
Liquid detergent
Food coloring
White tissue paper
Glue
Cardboard cut in desired shapes

PROCESS:
Pour room-temperature canned milk into a see-through glass cake pan so all can see from various angles. Add drops of food coloring and liquid detergent. Now watch the colors spin and merge in a rainbow array.

Take a piece of cardboard and smear glue on one side. Place white tissue paper on top (tissue paper should be a little bigger than cardboard), bunching up the paper so various lines and creases appear. Place the tissue paper over the top of the swirling designs very carefully and pick up the colorful images. Carefully wrap edges of tissue to the back.

Idea used with permission by Kevin Carnes who does workshops for Lakeshore.

FINGER PAINTING WITH YOGURT

MATERIALS:

Large container of plain yogurt

Containers to mix yogurt

Food coloring

Flavorings

Paper (We prefer using finger painting paper as it's smooth and the
    yogurt glides along.)

Examples: Mix yellow food coloring in a container with yogurt.
Add lemon flavoring.
Mix green food coloring in a container with yogurt.
Add mint flavoring.

PROCESS:

Take a large sheet of paper and allow the children to spoon various colors of yogurt onto their paper. It's fun to finger paint and taste the cool creamy yogurt. Hang to dry. It may take a couple of days to dry.

Note: Tabletops work great for finger painting. Have the child place a sheet of paper on top of his artwork, rub gently and transfer the design onto the paper. You'll have a monoprint design that smells wonderful and tastes good, too!

GLIMMER WRAP

MATERIALS:

Aluminum foil (cut or tear to desired size)
Container of acrylic gloss medium and varnish (Glossy acrylic polymer can
    clean up with water, but it's expensive. Arts and crafts stores usually have it.)
Colorful tissue paper
Other optional ideas are glitter, diamond dust, thin strands of thread,
    small dried flowers
Containers for gloss
Brushes to apply gloss (wide brushes or sponge)

PROCESS:

Mix a very small amount of water with the gloss that you will be using. Tear or cut up tissue paper and brush gloss all over the foil. Arrange the tissue in the pattern you like, and let the gloss soak through. Glitter, diamond dust or thread can now be added. When dry, the results are dazzling. It makes wonderful wrapping paper!

Hint: It's possible to substitute a mixture of one part white glue to two, or three parts acrylic floor wax for the acrylic polymer, but the wrap will not be as shiny.

Note: If you are making wrapping paper, don't use dried flowers.

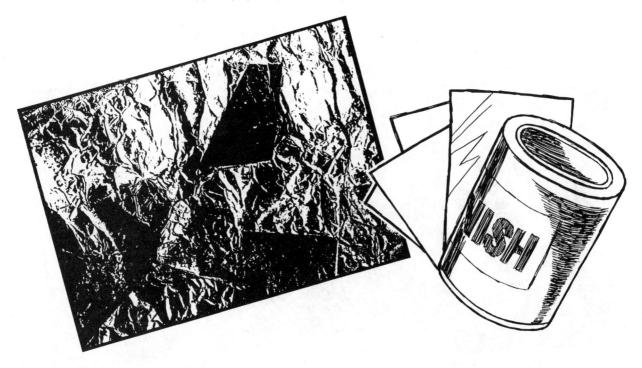

LIQUID PLAY DOUGH

MATERIALS:
Food coloring
Flour
Water
Salt
Squeeze bottles
Paper plates

PROCESS:
Mix salt, flour, water and desired amount of food coloring to the consistency of thick glue. More salt needs to be added than flour. The dough should come out of the squeeze bottles easily.

Squeeze designs onto the paper plates or corrugated cardboard. Relief sculpture can be achieved by placing another plate on top of your design and twisting and turning the plates with your hands in a "sandwich-type fashion." This project takes a few days to dry or can, if watched carefully, be placed in a warm oven for a few minutes. (Warm oven should be 100°F [37.7°C] or lower.)

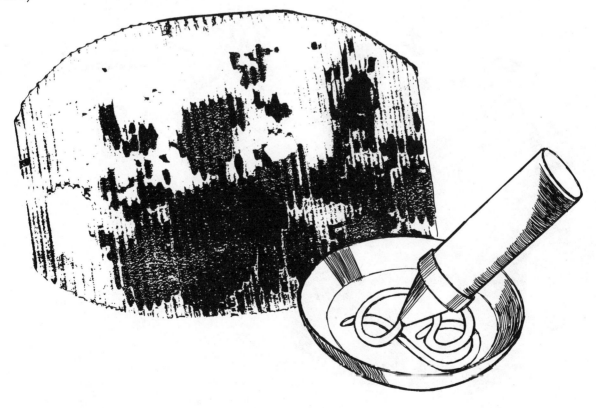

FOOD COLORING AND BLEACH

MATERIALS:
Coffee filters
Food coloring
Droppers
Bleach

PROCESS:
Make sure surface underneath is well protected when adding droppers of bleach, or place coffee filter in a plastic tub. Squeeze various drops of food coloring on coffee filters. Fill droppers with a small amount of bleach. (Bleach can be watered down a bit and close supervision is needed!) Squeeze dropper with bleach in a few areas of color. Watch colors separate and some areas turn white.

MAKING RECYCLED PAPER

MATERIALS:

Newspapers, comics, junk mail
Blender
Fine screen (can be obtained from a hardware store)
Old towel
Spoon
Rolling pin

PROCESS:

Place shredded paper in a blender with water. The ratio of water to paper is not that important; the mixture should be thick and gloppy. This is called the "slurry."

Lay a piece of fine screen on an old towel. Spoon some of the slurry onto the screen. Place another piece of screen on top. Roll with rolling pin.

Rolling forces the water out and presses paper particles together. Drying time will vary depending on the weather. When dry enough, peel the paper from the screen and allow it to dry completely.

Idea used with permission by Karen Stafford.

TUBE ART

MATERIALS:

Various kinds of tongs

Assortment of tubes (Tape one end closed with duct tape.)

Paper cut to fit inside tube

Variety of different sized balls with various textures such as golf balls, marbles, Koosh™
balls, racket balls, dog toy balls, etc. (Make sure these fit into the tube.)

Tempera paint poured into shallow containers

PROCESS:

Slide the paper into the tube. Have the children pick up a ball with the tongs and dip it into the paint. Drop the ball into the tube and covering the open end with a hand, shake the tube and roll the ball about inside the tube. Take the ball out and repeat the process with other colors and other balls. Various types of tongs with a variety of ball sizes and textures can make this a challenging, yet fun art activity. Remember, the finished product does not matter although there will be an interesting printed paper inside the tube to pull out.

Note: Wear a rubber glove if you don't want to get paint on the hand covering the open end of the tube.

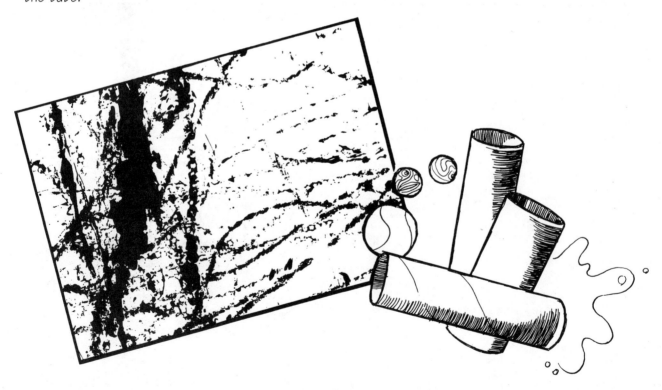

SALAD SPINNER ART

When my third son was two years old, and Kim and I had just completed our first book, I noticed my son's obsession with my salad spinner. He loved turning the handle and spinning it around and around. As I watched him, an art idea came to me. (Some of our best ideas come from watching children and really paying attention to what they like to do!) I thought to myself, why not add some paper and squirt some paint on it and give it a whirl? It reminds us all of the carnival spin pictures that we did as kids. What's wonderful about this art is that it is totally kid-powered. Using a large and a mini spinner, children experience two different gross motor skills—fine and large. This encourages children to cross the mid-line which is a skill that needs to be developed for prereading.

This is an art activity for which you will need to put out a lot of pre-cut paper circles. The kids love it!

MATERIALS:

Salad spinner (We like putting out a large and a mini spinner*.)
Paper cut into circles (Take out basket and trace the outer perimeter.) Use the
    kind of paper that is most accessible to you, such as construction paper,
    computer paper, butcher paper or coffee filters.
Small bottles filled with tempera paint or small bottles filled
    with colored glue
Optional: Glitter

PROCESS:

Place the circle into the basket of the salad
spinner. Fit the basket into the salad spinner.
Randomly squirt squiggly lines of paint or glue
onto the paper. Put on the lid to the
salad spinner and give it a
whirl. Take off the lid and
add glitter if you'd like.

*See supply list on
 page 136.

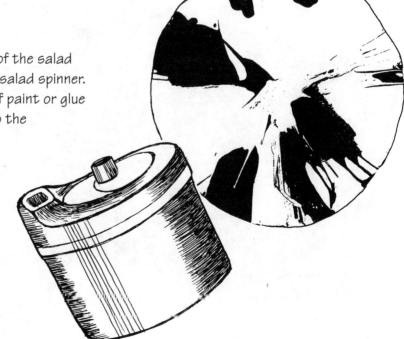

BEATER ART

MATERIALS:

Electric beaters or hand-held beaters
Good size unbreakable bowl
Paper sized to fit inside bowl
Assortment of at least two colors of tempera paint
Containers to put paint into so that it can be spooned into the bowl
Spoons or small ladles for paint

PROCESS #1:

Place the paper into the bowl. Spoon or ladle paint into the bowl. Turn the beaters on and whip the paint around and about the paper. Turn the beaters off and add additional colors. Continue beating the paint about until you have the pattern you want to achieve.

PROCESS #2:

Don't bother placing paper inside a bowl. This time, try placing the paper flat on a tabletop. Turn the beaters on and paint on the flat surface. Add additional colors when desired and have fun!

Note: This is one of the craziest art activities we've ever done, but the children love it! Just remember: It's the process that is important. Product results may or may not be spectacular—but it is FUN!

PAPER POTTERY

MATERIALS:

Plastic bowls or plates depending on what you want to make (Unbreakable bowls
   and plates work best when working with young children.)
Liquid starch, flour and water or wallpaper paste
Large jar of petroleum jelly
Lots of newspaper ripped into strips (small pieces work best)
Containers (large enough to easily dip strips of newspaper and take out)
Blunt knife (butter or putty)

Remember: When working with papier-mâché, allow several weeks to complete project. You will
be applying several coats of newspaper strips, and each coat needs to dry thoroughly.

PROCESS:

Smear petroleum jelly generously on the surface of the plate. If you are working on a bowl, turn
the bowl over so that you will be smearing the petroleum jelly on the outside of the bowl. Cover
with newspaper strips.

Using either liquid starch, a mixture of flour and water or wallpaper paste (purchased at a
hardware store or wherever wallpaper can be purchased), pour the mixture in containers. Dip the
newspaper strips and place them on the first layer of newspaper which has already been applied
with petroleum jelly. After applying the first coat with paste or starch, set aside and let dry.
Drying time with each coat will depend on how wet it is. Weather conditions can help the drying
time by allowing you to set the plates or bowls outside to dry in the sun. You should allow at
least twenty-four hours per coat to dry. You will need to apply at least five or six coats.

After completing and drying all coats,
an adult can take a putty knife or
butter knife to separate the plastic
plate from the papier-mâché plate or
bowl. Some trimming may be needed
around the edges. The side that has
petroleum jelly on it, will now need to
have a thin layer of newspaper strips
applied with the paste or starch. Dry
thoroughly.

Now the real fun begins. You are ready
to decorate your paper pottery! You
can use tempera paints or acrylic

PAPER POTTERY *(cont'd.)*

paints. You can put a high-gloss shine on it by purchasing gloss sprays at craft and hobby shops, or use clear nail polish. We often use the clear nail polish, but we apply it after the children have gone home. (Work with good ventilation as the smell can give you a headache.)

You can also decorate your plates with tissue paper. We like using Liquitex™ gloss medium for applying the tissue. When it's dry, you automatically get a shine. You can use starch or watered-down glue as well.

Cut tissue into 1" (2.54 cm) squares to make it easier to apply. If using watered-down glue or starch, you will probably want to seal the plate with clear nail polish or a gloss spray.

This art activity does take a lot of time, but the results and satisfaction are SPECTACULAR!

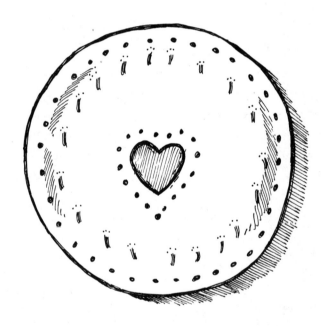

LINOLEUM SCRATCH ART

MATERIALS:

Linoleum squares
Crayons (big chunky ones work best)
Black latex gloss paint
Paint tray with roller
Assortment of nails, keys and other pointed and blunt objects
Acrylic floor shine (pour small amount into a shallow container)
Rag for smearing floor shine onto the linoleum
Blow dryer

PROCESS:

If you are working with small children, you may need to cut the standard linoleum square into a ¼ square. Too much area can be frustrating for a young child, and they will not be successful in covering their square with color. Color the square pressing down hard. Paint the colored square with the roller using the black paint. Using the blow dryer, dry the painted linoleum square. If you are uncertain about letting the children use something electrical, you could do it for them or let it air dry. The blow dryer is one of the favorite parts of this art. Once the black paint is dry, make a picture or pattern by scratching the paint with the nails, keys or other blunt objects that you might be using. The color will come through. Now rub some acrylic floor shine on a rag and cover the entire picture. This seals the picture and puts a nice shine on it. The blow dryer can again be used to dry the acrylic floor shine.

Some linoleum squares have peel-back paper and stick down. These are fun to let the children peel back and place down on a heavier tagboard square. Now their artwork is mounted on a border!

WALLPAPER PASTE ART

MATERIALS:
Tempera paint
Wallpaper paste (powdered form)
Toothbrushes
Cardboard

PROCESS:
Mix wallpaper paste with tempera paint. The mixture should be fairly thick. When you have mixed all the colors that you want the children to paint with, put toothbrushes in each container. Now give each child a sheet of cardboard to paint on. If you use powdered tempera, you will have to mix the paint and paste with water.

Have fun!

APPLE DIVIDER ART

MATERIALS:
Paper apple dividers (Most grocery stores have these and will give them to you for free.)
Tempera paint
Glue

PROCESS:
Sometimes teachers just don't realize what art resources they can find in the local grocery store! There are lots of different ways you can use apple dividers. Here are two ways the children in our preschools like to use them. One is to mix paint with glue and let the children drizzle paint and glue mixture on the inside of the apple divider. Another way is to let the children paint the outside of the apple divider with lots of different colors of tempera paint.

The apple dividers are also good for making collages. After the children paint the inside of the divider with the paint and glue mixture, they can stick feathers, ribbon scraps, glitter, colored rice, colored macaroni and other collage materials in the sections.

NEWSPAPER HATS

MATERIALS:
Newspaper (lots of it)
Masking tape
Glue
Items to collage with such as glitter, yarn, colored tissue, paint, watercolors, etc.

PROCESS:
Take a full sheet of newspaper, and put it on top of the child's head. Put two more sheets of paper on the child's head. Take masking tape and tape it around the child's head. You are now ready to roll the newspaper that is dangling over the child's face. Roll the paper towards the top of the child's hat. This is where you can have some fun with the paper by forming it into different shapes by the way you roll the paper. Tape the rolled paper to the top of the child's head. The children are now ready to decorate the hats with lots of different art mediums. They can paint with tempera paint or put watercolors in spray bottles and let them spray paint their hats. They can also glue glitter, tissue or yarn to their hats.

Optional Idea: Use the watercolors from Germany to paint newspaper hats. They are spectacular! You can order the watercolors from Discount School Supply. See the supply list on page 136 for more information.

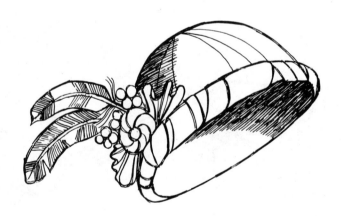

FACE COLLAGE

MATERIALS:

Small circles or ovals cut out or use small white paper plates

Scissors

Multicultural paints

Pictures of eyes, noses, mouths (Depending on your children's cutting ability, you
may prefer to cut these out ahead of time and place them in containers labeled
Eyes, Noses, Mouths.)

Glue

Scraps of yarn for hair

Optional: Make a hole at the top to put string or yarn through for hanging.

PROCESS:

Paint the small paper plate or circles with the desired skin tone. Let dry. This process can be
speeded up if you feel comfortable letting the children use a blow dryer to dry the paint.

Glue down the eyes, nose and mouth of your choice. Let the children have fun and be imaginative.

We have seen a dog nose with small squinty eyes and a big mouth. Heavily made-up eyes with a
huge nose and a mouth with a tongue hanging out—the possibilities are endless! Imagination
and creativity can really run rampant. Add eyebrows, hair, braids, ponytails, hair bows, ears and
earrings!

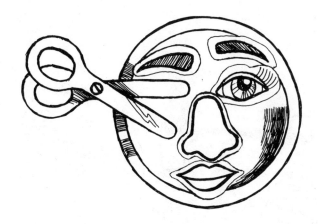

RAIN STICKS

MATERIALS:

Heavy tubes (I like to get the ones that postal supply places have for posters.
  They have lids that come off at each end. You can use heavy gift wrap tubes and tape
  the ends shut. The true test of durability is whether the tube can withstand hammering
  small nails into it. Make sure the tube is a length that can be easily maneuvered by
  whoever will be using it.)

Sack full of nails (I use drywall nails that are about 3½" [8.87 cm] long. The size and
  number you will need will depend upon how wide and how long your tube is. Nails
  should not poke through the opposite side.)

Small hammer

Sack of aquarium gravel, rice or split peas

Markers, tempera paints, watercolors, acrylic paints

Optional: Large roll of clear tape (used for packing)

PROCESS:

Decorate your tube with markers, paints or any other art medium you would like to use. When
dry, begin to hammer nails into the tube covering it top to bottom in random patterning. Tape
one end of your tube if it doesn't have a lid. Fill with ½ cup (125 ml) aquarium gravel, rice or split
peas. Cup the other end with your hand and roll back and forth. Do you want to add more
gravel? Do you need more nails? If you are satisfied with your sounds of rain, then seal the tube
at the other end with tape or the lid. You may want to tape around the tube with the clear tape
so the nails will not come out and the design will be protected. And now, let it rain, let it rain, let
it rain. . . .

BROOM PRINTS

MATERIALS:

Paper

Tempera paint

Large, deep containers for paint (You do not want to fill the containers with paint, just
cover the bottom enough so you can swish the broom around.)

Child-size brooms (You will need three or four brooms.)

PROCESS:

As Bev Bos advises, "It is important to honor what is natural in children." I feel that if we just
watch what children do, we can learn many ways of being creative. Broom art is one of those
ways—children love to sweep! They'll love it even more if you let them paint with brooms. This is
how it works:

Mix up four different colors of tempera paint. Give each child a large sheet of paper, or assign
several children to one very large sheet of paper. (This is great to do because you get the
children to work together.) You will want the children to do this art on the floor. That's what
makes it so much fun to do! Begin by taping the paper to the floor. Put the containers of paint
on the floor with a child-size broom in each container. Let the children paint on the paper with
the brooms. If you are unable to find child-size brooms, you may want to try using whisk brooms.
Be creative!

FURNACE FILTER PRINTS

MATERIALS:

Furnace filter (They come in assorted sizes at your hardware store.)
Paper
Tempera paint
Pie tins
Prepsicles* or sponge brushes

PROCESS:

If you find a terrific bargain (usually at the end of the season) you could let each child do his or
her own filter. Kim and I like purchasing a really big filter and putting it out as one of the art
activities for the day, letting children paint on it as a group—working together cooperatively.
Put out a stack of paper, and after they paint they can rub their painting and make a monoprint
from the filter. Some kids are just into dabbing on the paint and that is okay. It will dry and
another couple of kids will come along and paint and make a print if that's what they want to do.
After the day is done, you can display the colorful filter!

*See supply list on page 136.

PEPPER PAINTINGS

I recall an incident that occurred in my family when I was about 9 or 10 years old. Every morning my mother would make eggs for breakfast and something strange would happen. The eggs had blue and green dots all over them! We had mashed potatoes one evening and blue and green dots appeared on them as well! Blue and green dots began appearing on a lot of our food, and we were not sure whether it was safe to eat. My mother took some of our food into the health department so that we could solve the mystery. Well, as it turned out, containers of blue and green food coloring had spilled into a container of pepper. Every time my mother used pepper on our food, the color would vividly appear, sometimes to the point of disgustingly green with hues of blue. Recalling this memory, and knowing what a great laugh we all had once the mystery had been figured out, I decided to try an "art experiment" that was based on the pepper caper of long ago. The results are the art activity listed below. I seriously thought about calling this art experience AH-CHOO PICTURES, but neither I, nor the children doing the art have ever experienced the slightest urge to sneeze.

MATERIALS:

Large containers of black pepper granules
Pie tins or containers that are flat to help dry out the dyed pepper
    (Styrofoam™ trays work great, too!)
Food coloring (you do not need to use only blue and green)
Craft sticks
Containers that pepper can be easily shaken out of

PROCESS:

Into a flat container, place a generous portion of black pepper. Squirt food coloring randomly on top of the pepper. Stir with the craft stick so the color is evenly distributed throughout the pepper. Set aside and let dry. Repeat this process until you have several colors. Once the pepper is dry, empty each color into its own shaker. Test the container and make sure it shakes out easily. And now you are ready to make a pepper print!

continued on next page

PEPPER PAINTINGS *(cont'd.)*

OPTION #1 MATERIALS:

White construction paper (You are welcome to try other colors.)
Small squirt bottles filled with water
Colored pepper in shaker bottle

PROCESS:

Squirt the construction paper with water. Randomly sprinkle the pepper in the shakers onto the paper. Different colors will appear. (It reminds me of powdered tempera in the rain on paper.) Set aside and let dry. When dry, some granules of pepper will fall off.

OPTION #2 MATERIALS:

Container filled with straight liquid starch
Brush to apply starch
White construction paper
Colored pepper in shaker bottles

PROCESS:

Brush the paper with the liquid starch. Sprinkle the colored pepper onto the paper. Set aside and let dry. Some granules will fall off when dry, but the granules seem to stick better and seal better with the starch. Both methods have an interesting pattern effect.

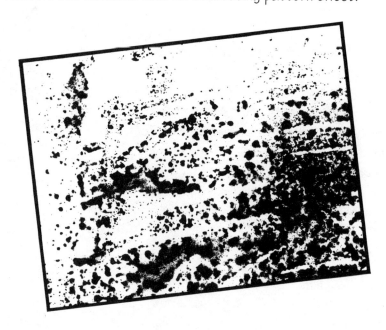

AFRICAN MASKS

MATERIALS:

Paper that is 65 lb. weight, linen finish (Paper needs to be 19½" (49.51 cm) wide by
   12½" (31.73 cm) tall. An office supply or paper goods store should be able to help you.
   You want heavy paper that can withstand wet materials that you will be adhering to it.)

Liquitex™ acrylic medium (Pour into container and add just a few drops of water.)

Brushes to apply medium

Assorted colors of tissue paper cut into small squares (This makes it easier for
   children to apply onto the mask.)

Assortment of beans, noodles (Noodles can be dyed before hand with food
   coloring.), feathers and sequins

Masking tape (to tape nose down)

Scissors

Stapler

X-acto knife (to be used by an adult)

Pencil

Full-strength glue

Optional:

Glitter

Egg cartons (Cut each section close and evenly to the bump so it can be applied
   easily for a nose.)

Elastic band (to keep the mask on your face)

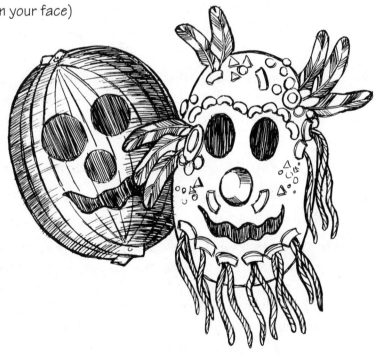

PROCESS:

Begin by drawing lines with a
pencil at each end of the paper.
Each line should be
approximately 4⅛" (10.46 cm)
long and 1½" (3.79 cm) apart.
You should have approximately
eight lines at each end of the
paper. If working with young
children, I would have these lines
pre-drawn. Cut the lines into
strips making sure that you only
cut to the end of the line where
your pencil mark is and that
each strip is even with the
others. Again, if working with

AFRICAN MASKS (cont'd.)

young children, you may want to have this all done ahead of time. Gather the strips of paper, working one side at a time. Place each end of the paper strip, one on top of the other until your reach your last strip. Pinch firmly and staple a couple of times making sure it feels secure. Do the same to the other end of the paper.

Now have the child place the mask up to her face and point where her eyes, nose and mouth are approximately. Make pencil dots as she points to each feature. Let the child draw the face with the pencil, incorporating the dots as placement to her facial features. Eyes can be overexaggerated as can all facial features. Teeth or fangs can be added, as well as eyebrows and grimacing lines.

To give a dimensional look, place the egg carton bump where the nose would be. Using masking tape, make an X with two strips of tape. The middle of the X should be the center of the egg carton bump. This bump will not show when you begin to tissue collage on the mask and cover it. The child may also choose to have a circle nose, oblong, etc. Let him choose since it is his mask.

An adult needs to cut the features out with an X-acto knife if it is too difficult or dangerous for a young child to do. The masks are now ready for the next step.

Using the bowl of acrylic medium, brush on the medium and place tissue squares all over the face of the mask. If younger children cover their eyeholes, nose or mouth—it's no problem. You can cut it out again when the tissue dries, or leave it as is.

Cover the egg carton bump (nose) and masking tape with tissue paper so you can no longer see it. The tissue will need to mold around the nose area. Younger children may need help with this. You are now ready for the next step in the process.

Use full-strength glue to add noodles, feathers, beans and sequins. This is where the mask takes on its own personality. Beans can be placed around eyes and other facial features. Interesting patterns can and usually do take place. Glitter can be sprinkled on as a finishing touch. Set aside to dry.

These masks can be strictly ornamental and hung up for display.

Optional: Using this mask pattern, make a jack-o'-lantern. There are many possibilities! Use your imagination and be creative!

Note: When Kim and I set up this art activity, we have various stations set up for children to move through. One table has the scissors, stapler and mask pattern. Another is a table with pencils, scissors and X-acto knives. This table will need adult helpers as they create their faces and cut them out. Then we have the "Nose" table that if they choose a dimensional nose, they can tape them right on. We have many rolls of masking tape, and we have pre-cut the egg

AFRICAN MASKS *(cont'd.)*

carton noses out. The next table is tissue squares, brushes and acrylic medium. The final station is glue with containers of beans, noodles, feathers, sequins and glitter. That makes a total of five stations. Children move about freely, and the air is filled with the humming chatter of conversation and creative involvement. It's a great environment of fun and open-ended creativity.

BUTTERFLY COLLAGE

MATERIALS:

Plastic sealable sandwich bags (You can use the quart or gallon bags if you want
to make bigger butterflies.)
Pipe cleaners
Collage materials such as hole punch dots (confetti), glitter, small paper scraps or strips
that can be colored on with crayons or markers, colored cotton balls, small dyed
noodles, bits of ribbon, string and any other bits of collage materials that you
have available
Containers in which to place collage materials.

PROCESS:

Have the children open up their plastic bags and place the collage items inside. Close up the
bag, squeezing out all the excess air. The Ziploc™ edge will appear on one side of the wings rather
than the top or the bottom. Gather the bag in the middle, placing collage items equally on both
sides. Pinching the middle, take a pipe cleaner and wrap it around so that it feels secure and
collage items are on both sides of the wings. Bend the pipe cleaner to make the butterfly
antennas. Your colorful butterfly is now complete. What a great way to use up leftover scraps
of paper and recycle items that you may have thrown away!

PORCUPINE FISH

MATERIALS:

Roll of aluminum foil

Tissue paper cut or torn into approximately 1" or 2" (2.54 or 5.08 cm) squares or rectangles

Container with liquid starch or Liquitex™ acrylic medium (if using the medium, add a little water)

Paintbrush or prepsicle* for applying the above medium or starch

Box of colored wooden toothpicks

2" (5.08 cm) Styrofoam™ ball

¼" to ½" (.6 to 1.25 cm) wiggly eyes (two for each porcupine fish)

Glue gun and glue sticks for applying wiggly eyes

Paper clip with fish line for hanging when completed

PROCESS:

Rip off a square of aluminum foil approximately 13" x 13" (33.02 x 33.02 cm). Cover the foil with liquid starch or acrylic medium. Place various colors of tissue paper onto the wet foil. Set aside and let dry.

Next, take the Styrofoam™ ball and wrap the foil around it, forming a flat tail on the end. Now would be a good time to glue gun the wiggly eyes into place. (You should do this for the child. We sometimes let the child just use regular school glue and then later glue-gun the eyes for a more permanent placement.)

Press colored toothpicks randomly into the Styrofoam™ ball. At the top of the fish, press a paper clip into the Styrofoam™ so that just a small amount of the clip is visible, and you can tie some fish line onto the hook for hanging.

*See supply list on page 136.

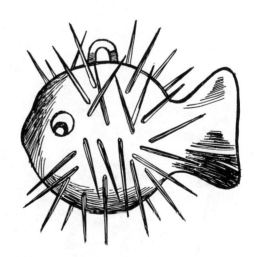

SPINNING TOP PAINTINGS

MATERIALS:

Assortment of tops (The party section in stores generally carries packages of these. Try to find tops that have a little pointy bump at the bottom. The round bottoms work too, but you definitely get different effects. Try both!)

Large sheet of paper (Butcher paper works great!)

Assortment of colors of tempera paint

Flat containers to pour paint into, putting tops into the various colors within easy reach

PROCESS:

Give yourself plenty of room to do this art activity. A table surface or floor works great. Take one of the tops that is in the container of paint, place it on the paper and give it a spin. Add another top with color before the first top stops spinning. Perhaps the second top will collide with the other and mix colors! Continue adding colors with additional spinning tops until you are satisfied with the results. The spinning tops fan out the paint depending how fast you can get them spinning. This is a great hand/eye coordination exercise.

Some children may have difficulty with spinning the tops. You can practice top spinning without paint just so they can get the idea.

Another option is to have a few children involved in making a large mural on the floor or table. Take a large sheet of paper and lay a Hula Hoop™ on the paper which will corral the spinning painted tops. You will want to have plenty of tops available so they can see how many they can get spinning at once (some pre-math skills?) and how many different color blends will be taking place. Overall, it is just FUN, and the results don't really matter. Children are working cooperatively, and I am sure there will be an exchange of much conversation and comradery.

PLASTER CASTING ART

MATERIALS:
Five rolls of plaster bandaging FAST SETTING (Can be purchased at a medical supply store,
   animal hospital or through Doodles and Oodles.)
Two small bowls of warm water
Cardboard
Watercolors

PROCESS:
Cut plaster bandaging into 4" (10.16 cm) long pieces. Give each child a small piece of cardboard. Let the children take the cut-up plaster casting and dip it into the bowls of water, and mold it on the cardboard any way they want. Now they can paint it with watercolors.

A variation of this is to let the children each have a 6" (15.24 cm) strip of plaster bandaging and dip it into the water. Instead of letting them mold it onto cardboard, let them mold and gather the plaster strip onto the table, let it dry for about fifteen minutes, peel it off the table and then let them paint it. Glue-gun a pin to the back and you have made a pin that looks like a flower and makes a cute Mother's Day gift! You can also buy plaster bandaging in different colors. If you buy different colored bandaging, it is fun to mold it onto cardboard, and drizzle black paint onto the colored plaster.

We think this art medium has endless possibilities for children to explore. We also feel it is important to take whatever art medium you are working with and let the children explore it as much as possible. They will come up with lots of different ways to use that medium. Remember, there are many ways of exploring art. Please give children lots of time at the art station!

CLAY VASES

MATERIALS:

Clay (low-fire clay can be found at ceramics shops)
Magnet ring and fishing line (to cut clay)
Paints (watercolors, acrylic, tempera)
Cookie cutters, straws, dry noodles (items with which
   to make impressions in the clay)
Newspaper
Masonite, 16" x 12" (40.64 x 30.48 cm) (the number of sheets will depend upon
   how many children you decide will be working at once—one for each)

PROCESS:

Clay is a wonderful art medium to work with, and there are lots of things you can do with clay. The wrap-around clay vase is one way of working with clay that can be a positive experience for children. You may want to call on parent helpers to assist with this project. Decide how many children you want to work with the clay at once. We feel four is a good number. Set up your masonite sheets so that the rough side is up—this is so the clay will not stick to the surface.

To cut the clay in 1" (2.54 cm) thicknesses, tie each end of a 16" (40.64 cm) piece of fishing line through the hole in a magnet ring. Push the fishing line down through the clay block. Give each of the children a piece of the clay that has just been cut. Let them roll it out into an oval shape with rolling pins. Don't let them roll it too thin, or their clay will rip when they roll it into a vase. Once the children make their oval shape, they can make impressions in the clay using cookie cutters, straws, dry noodles or anything that will make an impression. It is important the children do not cut all the way through the clay. When they are done making their impressions, they are ready to roll the clay into a vase. Take two sheets of newspaper, roll them into a cylinder. This doesn't have to be perfect. Take the clay and flip it over so the impressions are on the outside. Lay the newspaper cylinder on top of the clay at the bottom of the oval, and roll the clay around the newspaper until you get to the top of the oval. Now stand the clay up, pinch together the bottom of the clay so it can stand freely. You now have a wrap-around vase. Leave the newspaper in the vase, as it will help the clay dry faster. It will take three or four days to dry. When it is dry, take the paper out, and you are ready to take it to a ceramic shop to be fired. When you get the vases back from being fired, let the children paint their clay vases.

MODEL MAGIC™ CLAY

MATERIALS:

Crayola® Model Magic™ clay (can be found in educational stores or
    through educational catalogs)
Painting medium (bingo markers, acrylic paints, watercolors, markers of any kind)

PROCESS:

This clay is easy for children to work with and that is really important to us.
A two-pound (9 kg) tub will easily supply a classroom of twelve to fifteen children with some creative fun!

What you do with the clay is up to you. This is a very open-ended activity. We have a few suggestions that we have found very successful with young children and work with older kids as well.

Pinch Pots: Have children take a handful of clay and form it into a round ball. They then take their thumbs and press into the middle of the ball. As they press down, have them push out on all sides, and keep doing this until they get the size and shape bowls they want. If they don't like what they made, they can roll it into a ball again and start over.

Clay Pins: For Mother's Day we made pins which were a big hit. There are several ways to do this. One way is to let the children shape the clay into any shape they like for a pin. The other way to make a pin is to give them some clay, have them flatten it out and take different shaped cookie cutters and cut out whatever shape they like and paint it. When they are done, take some jewelry glue and glue a pin onto the back. If you would like the pins to be shiny, use clear nail polish and paint over their work. This also seals the paint to the clay. When choosing paint, stay with acrylic paints as they work much better than tempera paint. Tempera paint will crack and peel off.

SILICONE ART

MATERIALS:

Small piece of masonite for each child in the class
Two tubes of silicone bathroom tub and tile sealant
Two caulking guns for the silicone rubber
Glitter (many different colors)

PROCESS:

Make sure the handle is all the way out on the caulking gun, set the silicone tube into it and snip off the tip of the tube. Let the children draw with the silicone on a small piece of masonite. When they are finished, let the children sprinkle glitter all over their drawing.

A variation of this art is to let the children shoot the silicone onto the masonite, draw on it and let it set up overnight. Then let the children paint on top of the silicone base. Children can lay a piece of paper on top of the painted silicone, rub the paper with their hands and peel the paper off. The result is a print of the art that they did the day before. What the children seem to like about this art is using the caulking gun and being able to take their art home and paint it over and over and over again. It is a very powerful feeling for a child to be able to re-create something he made the day before.

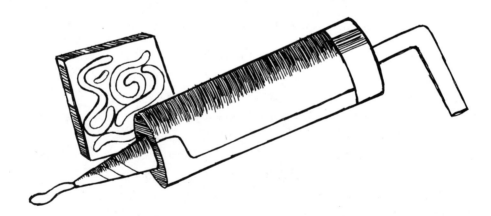

SILK PAINTINGS

MATERIALS:
Wooden embroidery hoops* (8" [20.32 cm] size or smaller)
Watercolors
Gutta Paint Resist™*
Small bottles
Blow dryer
Silk

PROCESS:
This is one of our favorite art activities! Not only is it fun, but it is easy for the children to paint and explore with this art medium. You will need to have silk stretched on hoops of about 8" (20.32 cm) in diameter. The silk size should be a couple of inches larger than the hoop size you choose to use. Take the piece of silk and put it on the embroidery hoop, tighten the hoop as tight as you can and pull on the silk so it is tight. After you have put the Gutta Paint Resist™ into bottles, let the children explore. Give each child a silk hoop and let him take the Gutta Paint Resist™ and draw with it. When they are done drawing, give them a blow dryer to dry their drawing. When dry, let them paint the silk with watercolors. Wherever they have drawn with the Gutta Paint Resist™, the watercolors will resist. The results are beautiful!

If you are uncomfortable letting the children use the blow dryer, you can do this step for them. If you cannot find silk at low cost, then try rayon.

*Silk hoops and Gutta Paint Resist™ can be purchased from Rupert, Gibbons & Spider, Inc. See supply list on page 136 for address.

UDDER ART

Last year my preschool class got hooked on cows after learning a song that Bev Bos had taught us "Many, Many, Many, Many, Many, Many Cows." Kim had a small cow table that we borrowed, and we were using it as a prop, when my assistant, Jeanette Anchondo, and I got an idea. We hooked a latex glove onto the wooden udder, filled the glove with water, put a small hole in some of the fingers, and let the children pretend to milk a cow. It was the closest we could come to the real thing at the time. Sad but true! The positive thing that came from it was a creative, fun art idea. We had been trying to figure out how to paint with these latex gloves, and thanks to my husband, Norbert, we have made this art a reality with an actual udder frame and base. Below are the directions and the process.

MATERIALS:
Pine wood that is ³/₄" x 1½" (1.91 x 3.81 cm)
Sack of disposable latex gloves (Gloves hang approximately
   16" [40.64 cm] from the base.)
Two 2" (5.08 cm) C clamps (Cost is approximately $2.00 each at a hardware store.)
Liquid tempera paint
Straight pin for punching holes in fingers of glove
Paper to fit inside base and under the udders

Build the base into a 2' (.61 m) square. The top portion of this fixture is a split design, tabletop sawhorse. The two parts of the sawhorse are clamped together to hold the latex gloves.

PROCESS:
Take two latex gloves and fill with liquid tempera paint. Add enough water so the paint is evenly dispersed into the fingers. Rubber band the top after filling, and place in container to take to the udder base frame. Unclamp the top and with a friend (it's easier with two), insert the glove and C clamp it at the top portion. The glove should dangle freely. Do the same with the other glove. Remove the rubber bands.

Lay a sheet of paper in the base frame. Puncture the glove fingers with a hole using a straight pin. You may want to make two small holes in the finger. I would puncture two or three fingers on each glove. Now you are ready to do art!

UDDER ART (cont'd.)

Pull and squeeze the fingers of paint as if you were milking a cow. Streams and dots of paint will come out, being controlled by the participant. Another child can work on the other color glove, and together they can create a picture! Colors will mix and blend. It's a fun, exciting process!

After the glove is empty, reopen the clamp and remove and discard. You could wash it out and use it again, or put it at a water table (after cleaning out the paint) and just play with filling it with water and squeezing the water out the holes!

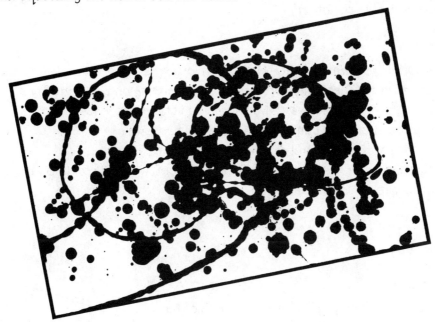

BACKPACKS

About fourteen years ago while I was working at a preschool, a parent shared with me an idea for making backpacks with grocery bags. I have no idea where the original idea came from, but it's a wonderful way to recycle grocery sacks!

MATERIALS:

Paper grocery sacks (To make one backpack, you will need two large, paper
    grocery bags—one inside the other)
Scissors
Duct tape
Two strips of material approximately 40" (101.6 cm) long by 2" or 3"
    (5.08 or 7.62 cm) wide (These measurements will depending on the size of the
    child. You may want shorter strips. Give yourself a little extra material to tie
    on the inside of the sack so it can be adjusted when needed.)
Rubber band or string for opening and closing
Two lightweight cardboard circles 2" or 3" (5.08 or 7.62 cm) wide (file folders work great!)
Stapler for stapling circles to backpack
Tempera paint
Paintbrushes
Containers for paint

PROCESS:

Using full-size brown paper bags, place one sack inside the other. Start cutting the back corner side of the sack, down about 7" (17.78 cm). Do the same to the other back corner side. (This cut goes down about halfway.) You should have a piece which I will call a flapper that you can now crease and fold down in front of you. Now with the remaining sack, cut the three sides that are tall to the height where the flapper folds down. The sack should now look somewhat like a rectangular box with a flap. Taking the flap, staple one cardboard circle a couple of inches from the bottom, in the middle. Lifting the flap, place the other cardboard circle approximately 2½" (6.35 cm) down from the middle and staple it in place. This circle is to be located in the front, middle section of your rectangular box shape.

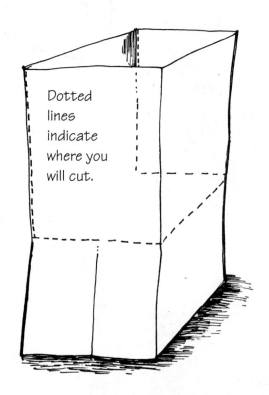

Dotted lines indicate where you will cut.

BACKPACKS *(cont'd.)*

Now you can cut a heavy piece of string and tie it around the circle on the flapper, leaving a

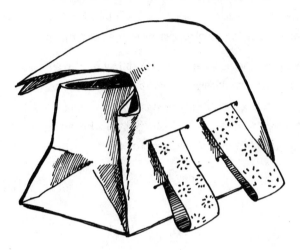

portion dangling to wrap onto the bottom circle for closure. We like using rubber bands as they do not seem to be as complicated for smaller children to use. Now you are ready to paint and decorate your backpack. Let dry.

Lift the flapper and make two sets of vertical slits in the back end of the backpack. On each side you will have one pair of slits. Each pair should be approximately 2½" (6.35 cm) wide. It will depend on the scraps of material that you will be inserting into these slits as to how long you will want to make your slits. I suggest going smaller to make sure it is the right length. You can always go back and cut longer lengths if needed. Insert your material strips into the top and bottom of the vertical slits and tie when adjusted properly to the child. You can tape the knot from your material strip to the inside of the sack with duct tape if it seems to have too much slack. Your backpack is now complete and ready to carry all those special items!

GOURD ART

Warning: This art is very contagious. You will start with the simplest form (using markers) and not want to stop! You will infect your family, friends and colleagues. Soon you will be checking books out on the subject and becoming an expert, making bowls, jewelry, ornaments and more!

The first weekend of August in Coeur d'Alene, Idaho, we have a festival called Art in the Green. It is put on by the Citizens Council on Arts, and in addition to art, there is great music and food. I mention this as there is also a wonderful "hands-on" art area for children and adults. This is where I was first introduced to the world of gourds. Many thanks to Thomas Orjala who shared his gourd knowledge with me and has gotten me hooked on this incredible art form!

MATERIALS:

Felt-tip markers and acrylic paints
Gourds that have undergone the drying process
   (explanation follows materials list)
Sandpaper (medium-coarse)
Detergent
Pot scrubber for cleaning surface of gourd
   (one with a handle works best)
Optional: Clear, shiny, gloss spray to put on when art is completed and dry.
   (This will protect the art surface.)

Preparing Gourds – The Drying Process

Gourds can be purchased year round through various hobbyists and commercial growers. You can obtain additional information and a list of gourd growers by writing: The American Gourd Society, Inc., P.O. Box 274, Mt. Gilead, OH 43338-0274.

You can grow them quite easily in your own yard if you have the space. Gourds do not deteriorate with age, so they can be stored in a dry spot in a basement, attic or storage room.

Whether you have purchased or grown gourds, they must go through a drying process before you can paint or use felt-tip markers. If the gourds are not heavy, you can hang them by their stems to dry. Otherwise just lay them in a dry, sheltered place on newspaper. Do not let them freeze!

After a few weeks you will need to turn them so air can get to all sides. They will more than likely get very moldy and gross-looking. This is what you want them to do, so don't

GOURD ART *(cont'd.)*

panic and throw them away. Mold doesn't hurt them unless they are totally mushy all the way through, and then they probably were picked too soon.

Gourds usually take two to three months to dry depending upon their size and the location that you are drying them. When dry, they need to be scrubbed to remove the outer layer of skin. It will take another day or so for the gourd to dry after washing. Detergent can be used to soak the gourds and make the skin (and mold) easier to remove. Using a pot scrubber, scrub the gourd to remove the skin. Some of the buildup can be removed with sandpaper after the gourd is clean and dried.

Now the gourd is ready to be painted or felt-tip markers can be used. The results are spectacular! Spray some gloss spray on your gourd if a high shine is wanted to seal your finished artwork!

This art is very nonthreatening to all ages, and gourds take on their own unique shapes that unleash different forms of creativity in everyone. One gourd may look like a snake coming out of a basket, a penguin or a wild animal. The long-handled ones can be made into maracas. Some can be made into birdhouses. With an electric craft tool, you can cut and etch into the gourds. Beautiful bowls and planters can be made. It is a fun art form for all!

"ME" DOLLS

A few years ago, our local college did an art activity with their preschoolers for their on-campus art show. They took the paper doll activity one step further. Using old sheets, they drew each child (front and back), stuffed each form with newspaper and sealed it with a glue gun. The following year we decided to do the same thing with my preschool class, except we purchased some cheap muslin.

MATERIALS:
Fabric markers
Muslin
Access to a sewing machine or a volunteer who can help sew
Polyester batting
Optional:
Have the child bring clothing to dress his or her "Me" doll
Dressmaker marking pen

PROCESS:
You will definitely want plenty of time or helpers with this activity! Fold a piece of muslin so you can lay the child down on the folded fabric. With the marker, trace around the child (giving thought to the person who will be sewing who may not be able to sew in very tight, skinny areas). You can always overexaggerate a curve or cut around the finger areas as a whole hand. Then give each child a variety of fabric markers to color in their features, hair and draw an outfit if he or she would like!

The dolls are now ready to be cut, sewn and stuffed. Kids love to help stuff their dolls! To reduce the cost of polyester filler, ask each child to bring in a bag of batting for his or her own doll.

This immediately becomes a very special doll to sleep with and to pal around with. They can be washed if you use fabric markers and polyester filler.

Idea used with permission from Kristin Parker,
a preschool teacher at North Idaho College.

SPAGHETTI ART

Painting with spaghetti is another one of those art mediums that is a little on the wild side. You may be wondering what the objective is to spaghetti art. There is but one objective—Fun! Fun! Fun! If you have never let your children paint with spaghetti, get cookin'! This art medium is a blast!

MATERIALS:
Cooked spaghetti
Tempera paint
Pie tins
Tongs
Paper

PROCESS:
Mix a different color of tempera paint in each of four pie tins. Cook enough spaghetti for about 2 cups (500 ml) to be placed in each tin. Pour the spaghetti into the pie tins and mix with the paint.

Set the pie tins on a table, and give each child a sheet of paper. This is where it gets really interesting. Some kids will dig right in with their hands and start painting with it. Others will try to pick up one long noodle and paint with it, or they will pick up a bunch of noodles and paint with them.

I think what I like most about this art is listening to the children laugh about painting with spaghetti. If you don't want the kids to pick up the spaghetti with their hands, try giving them tongs. That can be fun, too!

THE DRAWING WALL

MATERIALS:

Colonial White bath panel
Nontoxic Dry-Erase™ markers
Two socks (old socks)

PROCESS:

Every school should have a drawing wall. The drawing wall is the best center I have developed for my preschool. The drawing wall is a 4' x 8' (1.22 x 2.44 m) sheet of Colonial White bath panel. I had it mounted to my wall in my preschool; then I put dry-erase markers out for the children to draw with. Boy! Do they draw! There are days when I have children come into the preschool who are so angry at the world and everyone in it, nothing seems to calm them except for the drawing wall. Those children will head straight for the wall, pick up a marker and start drawing. A lot of what they are drawing reflects what is going on inside of them; no matter what else is going on in the room, there will always be another child who will pick up on that anger. Before long, that child will be at the drawing wall, drawing next to the angry child, consoling him through his own art.

Art! What a powerful tool! Fred Babb once said, "Art is what kids do to survive in an authoritarian society."

You can find a sheet of Colonial White bath panel at your local building supply store, and it costs only about $15.00. If your wall space is limited, you can cut the panel with a power saw. I used nails to mount the panel on my wall.

It is important that you use DRY-ERASE™ markers. Using the wrong kind of marker can ruin your drawing wall. The markers come in a wide variety of colors, and for safety reasons, we highly recommend that you use the nontoxic markers. Old socks make excellent erasers.

JOINT COMPOUND

And you thought joint drywall compound was just for your walls . . . Every class should have a tub of this stuff in the cupboard. It's a wonderful art medium and very inexpensive. Buy it ready-mixed, save cardboard and you will have an art activity always ready to go! We have finger painted on tabletops, made monoprints and as you will read on the following pages, there are many other open-ended art ideas you can do with it. When not in use, just put the lid on tightly and put it away. Always keep a supply of tongue depressors around as they work well for spreading the compound on cardboard and making textures. Other textures can be achieved with hair picks, combs, forks, nails, etc.

Additional ideas with joint compound can be found in the Holiday and Gift Section (pages 114-126).

JOINT COMPOUND ART

MATERIALS:
Joint compound
Pieces of heavy cardboard or tagboard
Tongue depressors
Various items with which to make impressions in the compound (such as forks, brushes, cookie cutters, straws, etc.)

PROCESS:
Give each child a 6" to 12" (15.24 to 30.48 cm) square of heavy cardboard or tagboard. Place a glop of joint compound onto each piece of board. Using various tools, move and play with compound for desired effect. Food coloring or paint can then be added as well as collage items. It can take several days to dry thoroughly.

JOINT COMPOUND COLOR BLENDING

MATERIALS:

Heavy cardboard or tagboard
Tongue depressors
Bucket of ready-mixed joint compound
Containers with lids
Assortment of liquid tempera paints or food coloring

PROCESS:

Fill containers half full with joint compound. Add tempera paint or food coloring to each container. Stir each container of compound so that the color is mixed thoroughly.

Have each child smear a generous portion of the plain, white compound onto a piece of cardboard. Next they can add and blend the colors that have been premixed in the containers.

Depending on the weather and location, this can take several days to dry. During warm weather, if placed in direct sun, your color blending picture will dry in approximately one hour. During winter and damp days, the same picture may take two days to dry.

JOINT COMPOUND WITH STRAWS

MATERIALS:

Heavy cardboard or tagboard
Bucket of ready-mixed joint drywall compound
Tempera paint
Tongue depressors
Plastic straws
Shallow pan or container to put paint into and dip straws

PROCESS:

Cover the cardboard with a thin layer of the compound using the tongue depressors. Don't spread it on too thick unless you want to let it dry overnight. You can work with the compound wet. Dip one end of the straw into the paint; then press it down into the compound to make a print. For smaller hands you may want to cut the straws in half to make it easier for them to make straw prints. Do not leave the straws in the compound. Use them for making colored circle patterns.

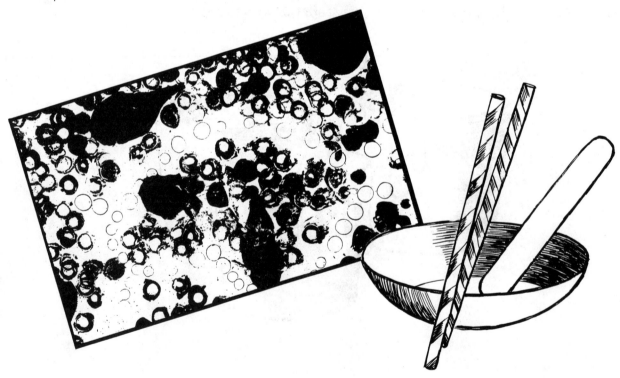

JOINT COMPOUND WITH TISSUE PAPER

MATERIALS:

Tub of ready-mixed joint drywall compound
Cardboard cut into desired shapes
Tongue depressors
Tissue paper cut or torn into desired collage shapes and sizes
Use one of the following to adhere to the tissue: watered-down glue, starch,
　　Liquitex™ acrylic medium with a little water added (if using 2 tablespoons [30 ml]
　　medium, add ½ teaspoon [2.5 ml] water)

PROCESS:

Spread a generous portion of joint compound onto the cardboard shape. Using the tongue
depressor, interesting textures can be created. Set aside and let dry overnight.

Brush on the substance you will be using to adhere the tissue. Sponge brushes work well. Stick
the tissue on randomly, full coverage isn't necessary. Some of the tissue will bleed color and add
to the overall creative look. Glitter or diamond dust can be added while still wet. Dried flowers
can be laid between layers of tissue for another effect.

JOINT COMPOUND WITH COOKIE CUTTERS

MATERIALS:
Heavy cardboard or tagboard
Tongue depressors
Bucket of ready-mixed joint compound
Assortment of cookie cutters—all shapes and sizes
Tempera paint, watercolors, colored glue
Brushes

PROCESS:
Spread the joint compound over the surface of the cardboard shape. Do not make it too thin or you will not get a good impression. Press the cookie cutter into the joint compound, placing your patterns randomly. Set aside and let dry overnight.

When dry, you can paint your picture with tempera, watercolors, colored glue, etc.

JOINT COMPOUND WITH CHALK

MATERIALS:

Tub of ready-mixed joint compound
Heavy-duty cardboard cut into desired shapes
Buttermilk or starch
Small container (deep enough for dipping)
Colored chalk
Tongue depressors

PROCESS:

At least twenty-four hours before you begin this project, smear a generous portion of joint drywall compound onto a piece of cardboard. Use a tongue depressor to make various lines and textural crevices. Set aside and let dry thoroughly.

Pour buttermilk or starch into a small container. Take a piece of chalk, dip it into the starch or buttermilk and begin coloring various areas of joint compound. Be generous with color and always dip the chalk into the buttermilk or starch. This helps to stabilize the chalk and works similar to an oil pastel.

Optional: Liquitex™ acrylic medium or acrylic floor wax can be smeared or brushed on after the chalk dries. A shine brings out the richness of the colors and seals the art with a protective coat.

JOINT COMPOUND WITH PLASTER CASTING

MATERIALS:

Heavy cardboard
Tub of ready-mixed joint compound
Tongue depressors
Rolls of plaster casting*
Liquid watercolors, food coloring, watered-down tempera paint
Pipettes* or eyedroppers
Scissors for cutting casting or have it cut ahead of time

PROCESS:

Prepare the cardboard ahead of time by spreading a generous portion of joint compound onto the cardboard. Cover the entire shape and add various textures with the tongue depressors. Set aside and let dry overnight.

Fill a shallow container or bowl with warm water. Dip the plaster casting squares into the water and place in various areas on the dry joint compound. Interesting structural peaks can be easily achieved, and when dry, the picture will have depth and texture. After placement of the plaster casting squares, set aside and allow to dry. They set up quickly. You can also begin to paint while it is still wet. Using eyedroppers or pipettes, fill with a variety of colors using watered-down paint, food coloring or liquid watercolors. We like using Neatness Jars, which are plastic paint pots that have six little containers all connected into a base with six lids. You can order these through the supply list in the back of this book, or you can use muffin tins or any other small container that won't tip with an eyedropper hanging out of it.

*See supply list on page 136.

JOINT COMPOUND WITH RELIEF MAPS

MATERIALS:

Heavy cardboard or tagboard
Bucket of ready-mixed joint compound
Smaller pieces of cardboard for placement of additional structures
Craft sticks, tongue depressors
Tempera paint, watercolors
Small pebbles or aquarium rock
Toothpicks
Construction paper

Optional:

Milk cartons of assorted sizes to be made into houses and covered with joint
    compound after windows and doors have been cut out
Pointy paper cups cut to use as mountain ridges, volcanoes
Dried moss to be added when compound is wet or glued on after drying

PROCESS:

Spread the joint compound onto the cardboard shape. Textures can be added as you create the terrain. Pebbles or aquarium rock can be used to make a rocky area. Create rivers with a craft stick or pencil top by pulling through the compound. Trees can be created with toothpicks and construction paper. Possibilities are endless. Make dinosaur terrains that you can add dinosaurs to after it is painted. Create animal habitats. Try a jungle with a family of monkeys on tiered rocks; a desert with cactus, snakes and coyotes; a mountainous terrain with a cave and a bear with her cubs; or an ocean scene with a sandy beach and jagged coastal terrain with a spouting whale in the ocean. All that is needed in this art activity is creative time and imagination.

You may want to begin the terrain, and create the structures while the joint compound is wet. Then glue on more when the compound has dried. You can always add more compound to various areas.

Shine can be added by brushing on Liquitex™ gloss medium or spraying a gloss sealer that can be purchased at a craft or hardware store.

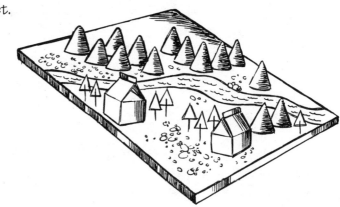

JOINT COMPOUND WITH BINGO MARKERS

MATERIALS:

Tub of ready-made joint compound
Tongue depressors
Heavy-duty cardboard cut into desired shapes
Bingo markers in an assortment of colors

PROCESS:

Smear a generous layer of compound onto the cardboard with a tongue depressor. The texture of the surface can be creative in itself, but do bear in mind that peaks can be difficult for the sponge applicator on the bingo markers. Set the cardboard with the compound aside, and let it dry overnight.

When dry, press bingo marker directly onto the compound. If a high shine is desired, Liquitex™ acrylic medium can be applied with a sponge brush or small cloth.

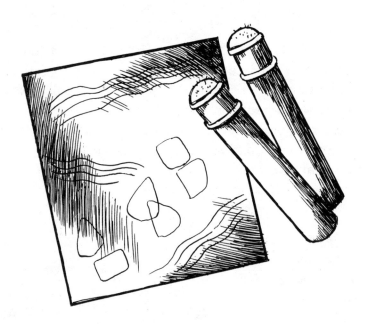

JOINT COMPOUND FOREST AND COTTAGE

MATERIALS:

Heavy tagboard or cardboard
Bucket of ready-mixed joint compound
Box of graham crackers
Box of ice-cream cones—the kind with pointed bottoms work best
Assortment of candies
Tempera paint
Craft sticks and tongue depressors
Ready-mixed frosting

PROCESS:

Spread a generous portion of compound onto the cardboard. Take the graham crackers and begin building your cottage using the compound as a glue to seal seams and build your roof. Pathways and textural surfaces can be easily achieved now while the compound is wet and easily slides about. If desired, use a craft stick to mix up a portion of compound in a container with green tempera paint. This can be blended into the already-spread compound for grass, or mix brown paint into compound for ground, blue tempera paint for water, etc. You may want to build a fence with craft sticks stuck into the ground.

To add trees, take a pointed ice-cream cone and coat the outside of the cone with compound. The mixture of compound with green tempera paint can be blended onto the tree at this time. This is easier to do now while the tree can be placed onto your finger. Make sure when positioning your tree, that there is a substantial amount of compound underneath it and around the tree. If a winter scene is being depicted, plain compound can be added with green peeking through to look like snow-capped trees. Set your cottage and forest to the side to dry overnight.

When thoroughly dry, you can decorate your cottage and landscape with candies. Using the ready-made frosting, adhere the candies to the cottage and roof, or use them to make a candy fence. *Do not adhere candy to wet joint compound. It causes the candy to melt, and you will have a wet, oozy mess in a very short time.*

JOINT COMPOUND MARDI GRAS MASK

MATERIALS:
Poster board cut into desired shapes
Tongue depressors
Bucket of ready-mixed joint compound
Dowels (³⁄₈" [.95 cm] diameter cut in 12" [30.48 cm] lengths)
Glue gun and glue sticks
Art materials that you will be using on your mask will be determined by the art medium that
you choose. After explaining the process, we will suggest some art mediums that will list
the materials.

After deciding what shape your Mardi Gras mask will be, cut out the size eyeholes that you'd
like. Spread a thin layer of joint compound onto the poster board using a tongue depressor. Let
dry for twenty-four hours.

Note: If you will be using the art medium **chalk and buttermilk,** make circular movements
across the mask with a craft stick into the joint compound so it will dry with this textural
effect. See "Joint Compound with Chalk" on page 103 for details on how to use this art medium
if you are unfamiliar with it.

After drying, you can choose the art medium that you would like to use or set
up a couple of different mediums, and let the children choose the one
that they would like to do.

Some suggestions are:

Bingo Markers: Glue feathers, glitter and
sequins on it once the bingo markers dry.

Tissue Paper: See "Joint Compound
with Tissue Paper" on page 101.
Glitter, sequins and feathers can
also be added with glue.

Tempera Paint or Acrylic Paint: When
dry, you can add shine by applying clear nail
polish or Liquitex™ gloss medium. Feathers, glitter and sequins can
then be applied with full-strength glue.

Cut wooden dowels into the length that will be easiest held by a child. On the
inside of the mask, use a glue gun and apply a layer of glue at the base. Lay
approximately ¼ of the dowel in the glue with the rest of the dowel hanging freely at
the bottom.

FISH PLATE PRINTS

MATERIALS:

Plastic fish plates*

Assortment of tempera paints—fluorescent colors are spectacular!

Butcher paper (Construction paper can be used, but butcher paper wraps around
   the curved plate easier.)

Brushes (We like using prepsicles*.)

Containers for paints

Optional: Bowl of soapy water and a rag to wash off plate for
   next participant

PROCESS:

Paint the plate entirely with desired colors. Have the child lay a piece of paper over the top and rub to make print. Carefully pull off paper and, voilá, a beautiful fish print without the smell.

*See supply list on page 136.

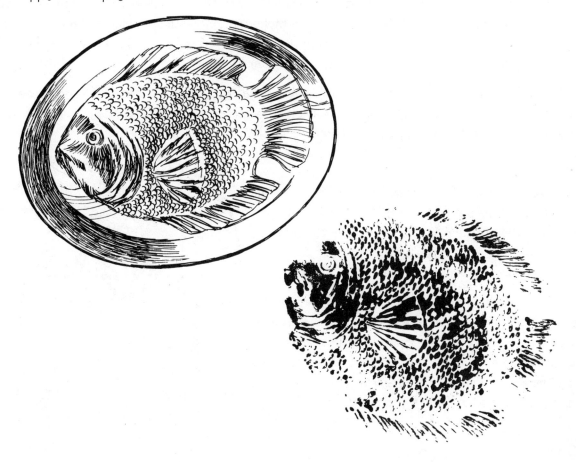

FISH PLATE T-SHIRTS

MATERIALS:

Plastic fish plates*
Fabric paint
Cotton T-shirt that has been prewashed
Brushes or prepsicles*
Cardboard to insert into T-shirt to prevent bleeding of paint to
   back side
Optional: One large wiggly eye, tube of white fabric paint for
   adhering eye to fabric

PROCESS:

Before you begin to paint the fish plate, on a nearby clean surface, lay the T-shirt front side down. Place your hands inside the shirt. They should be sandwiched inside the shirt so the palms are flat at the front portion, and the back of your hands should have the back portion of the T-shirt resting on top of them. Lift up your hands with the shirt as if you are ready to place the front center section on the plate to make a monoprint. You will be rubbing with your hands to transfer the print. Make sure you feel comfortable with this before you begin as you will be working quickly so the paint will not dry before you make a print.

Paint the fish plate with the desired colors covering the entire plate. Be sure all surfaces are still wet, or you may need to retouch a portion if it has dried. Picking up the shirt as described above, rub the surface of the plate with both hands. Work quickly, depending on the paint you use, the shirt will become very absorbent. You will want to get the cardboard inserted immediately so the back of the shirt will not touch the paint that may be starting to come through. When rubbing the plate to make the print, be sure to press down and rub on the entire plate to ensure you are picking up the gills, fins and eye.

If you like, add an eye by squirting some white fabric paint on the back of a large wiggly eye and mounting it where an eye would be. Don't put on so much paint that it squishes out when you press it into place. Let the shirt dry overnight. These shirts wash beautifully, but if you stick on a wiggly eye, don't put it in the dryer.

*See supply list on page 136.

FISH BANNERS

MATERIALS:

Plastic fish plates*

Muslin material cut into desired size and shape or
flour sacks cut appropriately

Dowels cut a little longer than banner (You can glue-gun dowel and fold over
banner at top as if sewn, or you can sew a strip at the top according to dowel
size to insert.)

Tempera paint (If you want the banner to be washable, you must use fabric paints.)

Brushes or prepsicles*

PROCESS:

Paint the plate with desired colors. Laying the material over the top, rub. Pull off carefully and
set aside to dry. When dry, dowel can be inserted.

*See supply list on page 136.

FISH PLATES WITH CLAY

MATERIALS:
Plastic fish plates*
Low-firing clay
Petroleum jelly
Glazes or paints
Kiln or access to one

PROCESS:
Roll the clay out about ½" (1.25 cm) thick. Smear a generous portion of petroleum jelly onto the fish plate. Place the clay on top of the plate, and press down all over the plate to ensure the impression will take. Leave the clay on the plate for at least one day. Gently pull off and set aside to dry—approximately three days. When dry, it will need to be fired in a kiln.

Now you can paint with glazes, and when dry, it will need to go back and be refired. If you do not want to refire, you can paint the plate with acrylic paint and put a shine on it with a gloss spray.

*See supply list on page 136.

STUFFED FISH

MATERIALS:

Plastic fish plates*
Tempera paint (or fabric paint if you want it to be washable)
Brushes or prepsicles*
Polyester fill, old socks or rags
Sewing machine
Muslin material
Scissors

PROCESS:

Cut the material into two squares that are bigger than the fish plate. Leave a margin around the fish, and figure you will sew a seam around the margin. Paint the fish plate with the desired colors. Place the muslin square onto the fish plate, and press to make the print. Repaint the plate and press the other muslin square onto the plate to make the second print. Set aside to dry. When dry, place the two painted fish together so they match up head to head and tail to tail, and the painted sides face each other. Sew around the margin of the fish, but leave an opening big enough to allow the child to help stuff. Turn the fish right-side-out so the painted side is now exposed. The fish is ready to be stuffed and hand-stitched closed.

*See supply list on page 136.

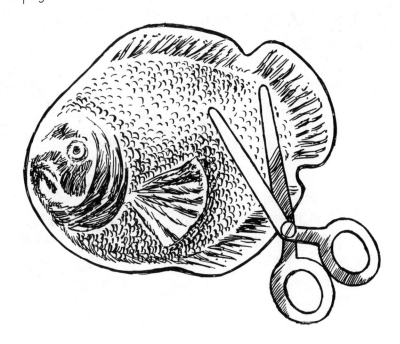

JOINT COMPOUND BALL ORNAMENTS

MATERIALS:
Styrofoam™ ball (The size should be appropriate for an ornament—I would
    recommend at least a 1½" to 2" [3.79 to 5.08 cm] ball.)
Joint compound
Tongue depressors or craft sticks
Paper clip for hook for hanging

PROCESS:
Depending on the medium you will be working with, you may want to plan on extending this
activity for two days.

Push a paper clip into the top of the Styrofoam™ ball leaving a small amount of the clip peeking
out so you can later attach a hook, string, fish line, etc. Smear the Styrofoam™ ball with joint
compound using a craft stick or tongue depressor. Make lots of textural swirls and rivulets.
Allow to dry overnight. If you prefer to work with the joint compound wet, refer to "Joint
Compound Color Blending" (page 99), or drizzle watercolors on wet joint compound with
eyedroppers or pipettes*. Allow to dry by hanging up freely.

If you will be working with the joint compound ball that has dried overnight, you can use several
art mediums to enhance this project.

MATERIALS FOR TEMPERA PAINTING:
Assorted colors of tempera paint
Brushes to apply paint
Containers for paint
Optional:
Acrylic gloss medium
Glitter or diamond dust

PROCESS:
Paint the joint compound ball with tempera paint.
Allow to dry and then for a high gloss, apply the acrylic
gloss medium. Use a rag or brush to apply the gloss
medium. While the gloss is wet, glitter or diamond
dust can be applied.

JOINT COMPOUND BALL ORNAMENTS (cont'd.)

MATERIALS FOR CHALK AND BUTTERMILK ART MEDIUM:

Small carton of buttermilk
Container for buttermilk (small margarine tub or bowl works great)
Colored chalk
Optional: Acrylic gloss medium

PROCESS:

Dip the chalk into the buttermilk, and color the joint compound ball. Press hard and make the colors dark, paying special attention to the areas that have swirls and rivulets. The contrast of color is especially brought out when applying the gloss medium with a rag.

*See supply list on page 136.

VOTIVE CANDLE HOLDERS

MATERIALS:
Tagboard

Scissors

Pencil

Box of votive candles or tea lights (The candle usually sits inside a metal circle base.
   USE CANDLES WITH METAL BASE ONLY!)

Masking tape, double-faced tape or use a glue gun to adhere the metal base and candle

PROCESS:
Draw a pattern that you will use to duplicate. Cut out the pattern from tagboard. Example: star shape. Listed below are options to decorate your votive candle holders.

Bingo Markers: Have the children bingo marker the cutout pattern. While the bingo marker paint is still wet, glitter can be sprinkled on. Glue-gun or tape the metal base holder with the candle onto the center of the shape or wherever the candle would seem the most appropriate.

Glue and Glitter: Draw a design onto the cutout pattern. Sprinkle on glitter. Adhere the candle and base as stated above.

Joint Compound: Have about four containers with lids available. Margarine tubs work great! Put a portion of joint compound into each of the containers. Decide if you want to use food coloring or tempera paint, and add a small amount of color to each container. Stir well with craft sticks or tongue depressors.

Smear the tagboard shape with joint compound, leaving an indentation where the metal holder and candle will be placed. You may find it easier to cut out a circle to place the candle into the shaped frame.

Blend the colors into the joint compound using the tongue depressors or craft sticks. You may want to create an interesting textural surface by dragging a nail or small comb through the wet joint compound. When dry (usually 24 hours), you may want to smear some acrylic gloss medium on the surface for shine.

VOTIVE CANDLE HOLDERS *(cont'd.)*

If you want to extend this project, smear the joint compound on the tagboard shape and let dry overnight. If you make swirly grooves with the craft stick while the joint compound is wet, you can create interesting markings that can be colored in when dry with colored chalk that has been dipped in starch or buttermilk. By dipping the chalk into the starch or buttermilk, you stabilize the chalk so it won't brush away, and it makes it a creamy chalk stick—like a stick of oil pastel. When dry, a small amount of acrylic medium can be smeared onto the surface. It provides a wonderful glossy shine and really brings out the colors!

After smearing the joint compound and letting it dry, you can bingo marker onto the dry joint compound (you will want a smoother surface for this). You can then add the acrylic medium for a spectacular shine. Don't forget to add your candle and base!

Optional Ideas: Tempera paint (use pencil tips or straws dipped into paint), watercolors, markers and colored glue. Some patterns look great being laid one on top of the other, like the star pattern below. Just glue on an additional star pattern, turning the star on top so that the points are in the open spaces.

BAR SOAP PAINTINGS

Doodling with a regular bar of soap can be an artistic endeavor! Dealing with ordinary household items can bring out the creativity within you. Art is all around—just waiting to be discovered!

With this particular art, a simple drawing awaits a splash of color to come alive!

MATERIALS:

Bars of soap
Construction paper
Assortment of tempera paint
Containers for paint
Brushes

PROCESS:

Take a clean, dry bar of soap and draw a picture on your paper. Brush off excess soap, and then paint the picture with tempera paints. Your picture will appear through the paint! This art smells wonderfully clean!

Have each child bring in a bar of soap. See how many different colors of soap are brought in. Each soap has a different smell. Discuss the different scents. When the children are done with their art, they can use their bars of soap to clean up.

MAKE YOUR OWN BUBBLE WANDS

Bubbles

Dip your pipe,
And gently blow.
Watch the tiny bubbles grow.
Big and bigger,
Round and fat,
Rainbow colored,
And then
SPLAT!

Author Unknown

MATERIALS:

Wooden dowels ³⁄₁₆" to ¼" (.48 to .6 cm) Cut these approximately 6½" (16.51 cm) long.
Plastic-coated copper wire (This comes in a variety of colors. It must be heavy
   enough to be pliable but retain its shape.)
Cookie cutters that have a lip to bend wire around
Wire cutters
Colored tape

PROCESS:

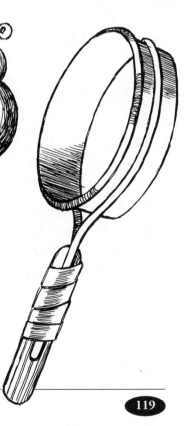

Cut off a piece of wire a little longer than the circumference of
the cookie cutter shape you will be using. Wrap the wire
around the outside of the cookie cutter, molding the
shape. Twist ends of wire to close. Remove the cookie
cutter. Hold the bottom end of the wire and wrap
colored tape around the dowel until the shape is
securely attached. Your wand is now ready to dip
into a bubble solution!

Note: This activity may be too difficult for young children
to master. They will need one-on-one help. It may be easier
for the child to make an abstract shape. We included this
activity because it is fun for teachers to have accessories for their
classrooms that are easy and fun to make and can be used
immediately!

Bubble Solution: Mix together 4 cups (1000 ml) hot water, 10
tablespoons (150 ml) sugar and ¾ cup (180 ml) Dawn® dishwashing
detergent.

ADHESIVE PAPER COLLAGE ORNAMENTS

MATERIALS:

Roll of adhesive paper (cut into the desired shape)

Collage materials such as cut-up ribbon, confetti, paper scraps, embroidery
thread, small feathers, felt scraps, etc.

Containers for your collage items

Backing for the adhesive ornament: wallpaper, construction paper, foil,
cellophane, wrapping paper (If you want the ornament to be see-through,
use another piece of adhesive paper.)

Scissors

Optional:

Hole punch for making a hole to hang ornament

String, yarn, paper clips or hooks for hanging ornament when completed

PROCESS:

Peel off the protective backing to the adhesive paper and begin collaging on the sticky side. Be careful to leave the outer edge free so it will stick to whatever backing you will be using.

Children love this activity because it's so easy for them to do. The sticky backing allows the easy placement of materials. Many young children love to play with the stickiness on their hands and then have the ability to release easily from the adhesive.

After making the ornament, depending on the age of the children, you may want to help them trim the excess paper from the adhesive. You will find it is much easier to have a bigger piece of backing than your adhesive ornament. Then simply trim around the adhesive pattern. Now your ornament is ready to be hung. These make wonderful sun catchers as well!

You can also make holiday place mats and gifts.

PLASTER CASTING ORNAMENT BALLS

MATERIALS:

Roll of plaster bandaging FAST SETTING (Can be purchased at a medical supply store, animal hospital or through Doodles and Oodles.)

Container filled with warm water

Scissors

Package of small, round balloons

Watercolors or tempera paint

Containers for paints

Brushes

Place to freely hang the ornament balls so they can dry (Clothespins work great with a string or vinyl line.)

Optional:

Glitter or diamond dust (Diamond dust is a clear sparkly glitter.)

Paper clip or ornament hook

PROCESS:

Blow up a small, round balloon and tie it off. Cut the plaster bandaging into approximately 2" (5.08 cm) strips. Dip the strips into the warm water and cover the balloon entirely, leaving the balloon tie-off end dangling. Hang the ornament from this end until it dries. It should be dry within a half an hour. Cut the balloon tie-off knot. This will release the air, and you can easily pull the balloon out and discard it. Your plaster ball ornament is now ready to paint! After painting the ornament, glitter or diamond dust can be added. Insert a paper clip or ornament hook into the hole where the balloon was pulled out. A bow can be added to camouflage the small hole.

You may also use this ball as a planet if you happen to be studying space. Let the child paint the ball with the appropriate colors of a particular planet, or let him create his own planet!

GLIMMER BALL ORNAMENTS

MATERIALS:

1½" to 3" (3.79 to 7.62 cm) Styrofoam™ ball
Aluminum foil
Assortment of tissue paper, cut into squares for easy placement
Sponge brushes or prepsicles* (These type of brushes glide more easily on the foil.)
Acrylic gloss medium
Container for gloss
Glitter or diamond dust
Paper clip or hook for hanging

PROCESS:

Cut a square sheet of foil so that it will easily wrap around the Styrofoam™ ball. Have the child spread the gloss medium onto the foil and apply the tissue paper. (Do not attempt to wrap the foil around the ball to apply this process.) Lay the foil on a flat surface, and wrap it around the ball only when the tissue paper has dried on the foil. We have tried it both ways and found it extremely frustrating for the children to place the tissue on a circular ball. You will have better success, and the children have more creative freedom working with squares of foil on a flat surface. While applying the gloss medium on the foil and applying the tissue, re-dab the tissue so the gloss medium has wet the tissue thoroughly to ensure that it will not fall off and a nice "shine" of color will emerge. Glitter or diamond dust can be added while the gloss medium is still wet. Drying will take about an hour depending on the weather and how wet the artwork is.

Once dry, the foil can be wrapped around the Styrofoam™ ball. Press in the paper clip, and it's ready to be hung!

*See supply list on page 136.

ICE CREAM ORNAMENTS

MATERIALS:
2" (5.08 cm) plastic foam balls
Box of sugar cones
Joint compound
Tempera paint
Tongue depressors
Glue gun
Paper clips

PROCESS:
You will need to glue-gun the plastic ball to the sugar cone. Mix up your joint compound with tempera paint. We usually mix four different colors to pick from. Stick a tongue depressor in each color. Give the children a sugar cone with the plastic foam ball glued in it, and let the children cover the foam ball with colored joint compound. If you would like to hang it up later, stick a paper clip in the top of the ball.

It is really fun to watch these ornaments being made. As the children start to cover the balls with the joint compound, they begin looking like real ice-cream cones, and the children begin licking their lips and asking when they can eat them!

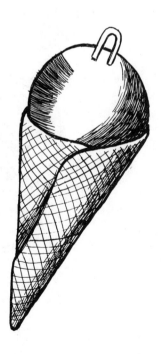

JUICE LID ORNAMENTS

MATERIALS:

Lids from frozen juice cans

White or colored poster board cut to fit inside juice lid. (Add a drop or two of glue if you
    want to ensure the circle will stay securely.)

Collage items such as macaroni, yarn, string, rickrack, seeds,
    glitter, etc.

Glue (Add food coloring if you want colored glue.)

Cotton swabs or brush to apply glue

Optional: Glue gun to attach string or cord for hanging

PROCESS:

Have the children glue and collage items in the poster board circle. Glue-gun yarn or string on
back to hang, or place a magnetic strip on back to make magnets for the refrigerator.

Optional Idea: Take a photograph of a child, and trace circle with a glass or form that will fit
into the juice lid. Cut out the photo circle and glue or rubber cement the backing to the juice lid.
Press with your nail carefully around photo edges to obtain a tight fit. Lace can be added
around the lid for an added "touch." Add a gold or silver cord glue-gunned to the back for
hanging. Makes wonderful Christmas ornaments! Write the date on the back, as this will be a
memorable item that will be cherished for many years.

TREE POTTERY

MATERIALS:

Low-firing clay
Access to kiln
Tempera paint
Optional: Diamond dust (clear shimmery glitter) or various colored glitter

PROCESS:

Take a ball of clay and form it around your index finger, pressing finger indentations into the clay. Pull your tree off your finger and tap the bottom of your tree on a surface to smooth the base (leave the hole underneath). Let the clay air dry for a few days, and then have it fired in a kiln.

After having the tree fired, you are now ready to paint the tree. White paint can be dabbled on to look like freshly fallen snow. While the paint is wet, add diamond dust or glitter.

COFFEE FILTER PRINTS

MATERIALS:
Coffee filters (flat or basket type)
Watercolor paints
Butcher paper
Muffin tins

PROCESS:
Squirt watercolors in each section of the muffin tin. Fold a coffee filter until you have a small square. Dip a corner of the filter into one of the watercolors. Dip another corner into a different color. Do this to all four corners. Let the watercolors bleed all the way up the filter. When you are done coloring your coffee filter, open it up and lay it down on a sheet of butcher paper. Do three or four more coffee filters the same way and lay them all down on the same paper. Now you are ready to lay a sheet of paper over the coffee filters and press down on the paper. The coffee filters will bleed through to the paper, leaving a really neat print. This paper would make great wrapping paper. The children love doing this activity! They think it's fun to watch the colors bleed together. They also think it is pretty neat to see the colors bleed onto another piece of paper.

Idea used with permission by Kristin Parker, who is a preschool teacher.

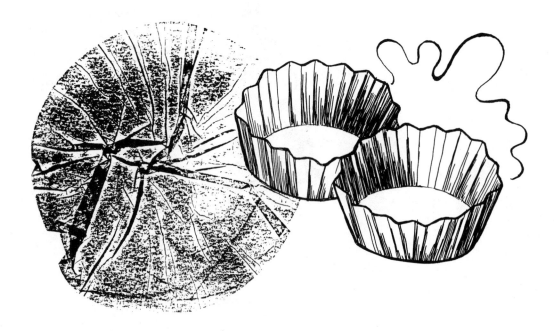

OUR FAVORITE PLAY DOUGH RECIPE

We are well aware that there are many play dough recipes in circulation, but this has been one of our favorites for the last ten years. If you do not have olive oil available, you can substitute another type of oil, but do try it with olive oil because the texture is wonderfully creamy. We usually double this recipe.

INGREDIENTS:
Water – 2 cups (500 ml)
Olive oil – 3 T (45 ml)
Food coloring
Flour – 2 cups (500 ml)
Salt – 1 cup (250 ml)
Alum (to preserve dough) – 2 T (30 ml)

PROCESS:
In a saucepan, bring water to a boil. Add the food coloring and olive oil. Remove from heat and add flour, salt and alum. Mix well. Knead the dough when the mixture isn't too hot. You may need to add additional handfuls of flour—play with the texture to make it the desired consistency. Place the play dough in a sealable container or plastic bag. Refrigerate if desired. If placed in an airtight container and not allowed to dry, this mixture can last up to three months.

FUNNY PUTTY

INGREDIENTS:
Glue (regular, not school glue) – 2 cups (500 ml)
Water – ¾ cup (187.5 ml)
Borax – 2 teaspoons (10 ml)
Water – ⅓ cup (82.5 ml)

PROCESS:
In a separate bowl or container, mix the borax and ⅓ cup (82.5 ml) of water. Make sure the borax has dissolved well into the water. Set aside.

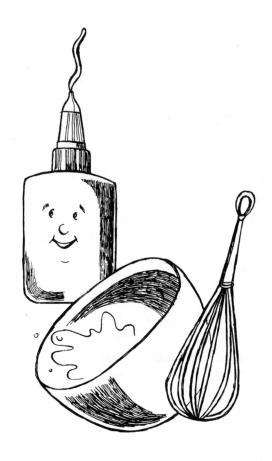

In another bowl, mix the glue and ¾ cup (187.5 ml) water. Add a few drops of food coloring if desired. Stir well and add container with borax and water. Magically, before your eyes, the mixture will begin to clot together. Knead. If excess water remains in the bowl, just leave it. This is a wonderful recipe to make with the children. They can play with it, pick up cartoons from the funny papers and it has a weird oozy effect when placed in small play dough molds and containers. Plastic forks are fun to use and make impressions into the putty because the impression disappears.

Put the funny putty in a large, resealable plastic bag, releasing the air. It will last approximately two weeks, maybe three, and then you will know it is time to be discarded as the smell gets to be rather persuasive. The end of the fun has come until you mix your next batch of funny putty.

GOOP

INGREDIENTS:

Cornstarch – 1 16 oz. (30 g) box
Water – 2½ cups (625 ml)
Food coloring
Plastic tub to mix this in and play with it in
    (Make up a larger quantity and put it in a
    kid-size swimming pool!)

PROCESS:

Empty box of cornstarch into plastic tub. Add
water and food coloring if desired and mix.
Add spoons, containers, small hand-held
shovels or just use your hands. It is a fun
substance to play with and is very
therapeutic! Children and adults will
play with this stuff forever! One
minute it is a solid in your
hand, and the next minute it
has slipped away and is a
liquid. You will want to
buy several boxes of
cornstarch so
you can mix up
a swimming
pool full!

SIDEWALK CHALK

MATERIALS:

Powdered tempera or liquid tempera
Water
Small waxed paper cups (5-ounce [150 g] size works great)
Plaster of Paris
Craft stick or plastic spoon
Measuring spoon (tablespoon size)

PROCESS:

I know of two different ways of doing this so I will explain both methods.

Dry Tempera Method

Mix 2 tablespoons (30 ml) powdered tempera and ¼ cup (62.5 ml) water in a paper cup with the stick or plastic spoon. Add 3 tablespoons (45 ml) of plaster of Paris. Stir well with stick or spoon. Consistency should be creamy. If not, add a little more plaster of Paris or perhaps a little more water if it is too dry. Mixture should feel hard in about an hour. Peel off the cup and you'll have a giant chalk stick to use on concrete. It works on a chalkboard, but it's not too spectacular.

Liquid Tempera Method

Mix 1 tablespoon (15 ml) liquid tempera, ¼ cup (62.5 ml) water and ½ cup (125 ml) plaster of Paris in a paper cup, and follow directions as above.

DIP AND DRAPE

MATERIALS:

1½ cups (375 ml) plaster of Paris
1 T (15 ml) alum
1 cup (250 ml) water
Cheesecloth or other fabric

PROCESS:

Mix 1½ cups (375 ml) plaster of Paris with 1 tablespoon (15 ml) alum. Add 1 cup (250 ml) water and stir well. Dip cloth into mixture and drape over form such as bottle tube, etc. Shape within 15 minutes. Add features.

At Halloween we made ghosts with this mixture using cheesecloth and bottles. The possibilities are endless. Just a little creativity and imagination are needed.

FINGER PAINTS

I have several recipes for finger paints which have been very successful. Finger painting is always fun and really allows you to be free and creative. We enjoy doing it on tabletops and making prints by placing paper over our creative marks and designs.

#1 INGREDIENTS:
Unflavored gelatin – one envelope (1 T [15 ml])
Cold water – ⅓ cup (82.5 ml)
Food coloring
Dishwashing liquid – 4 T (60 ml)
Cornstarch – ½ cup (125 ml)
Cold water – 2½ cups (625 ml)

PROCESS:
Mix the unflavored gelatin in a bowl with ⅓ cup (82.5 ml) water. Set aside. Put cornstarch and 2½ cups (625 ml) water into a saucepan. Stir to dissolve and bring the mixture to a low simmer. Mixture should be thickening. Remove from heat, and blend in the gelatin and water mixture with the cornstarch and water. Add dishwashing liquid. Let mixture cool and divide into containers adding desired food coloring. If any of the finger paints are left over after painting, you can store the mixture in covered containers at room temperature.

#2 INGREDIENTS:
Powdered tempera
Liquid starch

PROCESS:
Mix liquid starch into a container adding powdered tempera. Mix well, obtaining the consistency and color that you desire. Many times I just add a few spoonfuls of powdered tempera, pour in liquid starch and mix directly on the tabletop.

A few years ago Kim and I were in Seattle for an art workshop we were presenting, and we stopped off at the Children's Museum at the Seattle Center. We stumbled onto the newsletter they had and felt the information was so vital that we have asked them for permission to reprint it so that others may share in its value.

IMAGINATION STATION

Dear Parents and Adults:

Every child loves to make art . . . that's a given. If you are interested in continuing the creative development of your child in school you must begin now to address the lack of art education in our schools. Art certainly is fun for children of all ages, but the benefits of an art enhanced curriculum go far beyond the creation of a painting, a collage or a clay sculpture, or the appreciation of great works of art, music, drama and literature. Studies have shown that when art is an integral component of a school's curriculum, test scores, attendance, self esteem and grade points are higher than counterpart schools which have no art curriculum.

> "Recently publicized research in brain growth, learning styles, and critical thinking has indicated that the types of thinking, production and processing inherent in the arts are critical to the development of many children, while contributing to the overall growth of all learners."*

Besides fostering cultural enrichment, arts education has a practical application, the ability to foster creative and critical thinking skills. In this era of high technology, creative problem solving skills are integral to the invention and implementation of new ideas. It is not enough to offer math and science to address this new technology without the creative thinking skills that produce new ideas and inventions and solve problems. Currently in the U.S. fewer inventions are being patented than ever in our history. Can this mean that fewer people are thinking creatively?

What can you do? There are ways you can be an advocate for cultural enrichment and make a difference in promoting art education for your child's development. **Get involved with your PTA** and find out what kind of work they are doing to promote the arts in your child's school or the one she or he will be attending. If there are art specialists for your child's school or school district, **support them,** find out from them what's needed. **Contact other concerned parents and volunteer your time to make the principal, school board and the state legislature aware of the need for art education in our schools. Write to them, speak to them.** As you know, the schools are undergoing many changes these days, and it's important that parents be a part of this process. **Speak up for the creative potential of your child.** They need not become artists … indeed, the lasting effects of art education on a child are an enhanced ability to think, act and make decisions creatively whatever they do, as well as to appreciate the cultural achievements of all people.

For further information, contact the Alliance for Arts Education, 158 Thomas Street, Suite 6, Seattle, WA 98109.

*From the Washington State Comprehensive Arts Education Plan.

Reprinted with permission from Sarah Robertson, Program and Exhibit Coordinator, Children's Museum, Seattle Washington.

CALVIN AND HOBBES copyright 1992 Watterson. Reprinted with permission of UNIVERSAL PRESS SYNDICATE. All rights reserved.

FLOWERS ARE RED

The little boy went first day to school,
He got some crayons and started to draw . . .
He put colors all over the paper for colors was what he saw.
And the teacher said "What you doin' young man?"
"I'm painting flowers!" he said.
She said . . . "It's not time for art young man.
And anyway flowers are green and red. There's a time for
everything young man and a way it should be done.
You've got to show concern for everyone else
For you're not the only one."
And she said, "Flowers are red young man, Green leaves
are green, There's no reason to see flowers any other way
Than the way they always have been seen!"
But the little boy said, "There are so many colors in the
rainbow, So many colors in the mornin' sun,
So many colors in a flower, And I see every one!"
Well the teacher said, "You're sassy, there's ways that
things should be and you'll paint the flowers the way they
are . . . so repeat after me" . . . And she said, "Flowers are red
young man, Green leaves are green, There's no need to see
flowers any other way than the way they have always been seen!"
And the little boy said, "There are so many colors in the
rainbow, So many colors in the mornin' sun, So many colors in
a flower, And I see every one."

The teacher put him in a corner. She said, "It's for your own good
And you won't come out 'til you get it right and all
responding like you should."
Well finally he got lonely. Frightened thoughts filled his head.
And he went up to the teacher and this is what he said . . .
And he said, "Flowers are red, Green leaves are green.
There's no need to see flowers any other way than the way
they have always been seen!"

Time went by like it always does and they moved to another
town. And the little boy went to another school
And this is what he found.
The teacher there was smiling . . . She said, "Painting should be fun.
And there are so many colors in a flower, so let's use every one."
But the little boy painted flowers in neat rows of green and
red. And when the teacher asked him why …
This is what he said . . . He said, "Flowers are red, Green
leaves green, There's no need to see flowers any other way
Than the way they have always been seen."

Words and music by Harry Chapin
From the album *Living Room Suite*

SUPPLY LIST

- **Stamps, materials to make your own stamps:**
  A Small Woodworking Company
  Jim and Kathy Blodgett
  34207 82nd Avenue S, P.O. Box 460
  Roy, WA 98580
  206-458-3370

- **Exclusive dealer of BioColor® paints:**
  Discount School Supply
  P.O. Box 670
  Capitola, CA 95010-0670
  1-800-627-2829

- **Mini salad spinners, spiney balls, pipettes, prepsicles, plastic fish plates, plaster casting:**
  Doodles and Oodles of Art
  410 N. 20th Street
  Coeur d'Alene, ID 83814 or
  P.O. Box 1866
  Coeur d'Alene, ID 83816

- **Silk fabric, dyes, paints, Gutta Paint Resist™, and accessories:**
  Rupert, Gibbons & Spider, Inc.
  P.O. Box 425
  Healdsburg, CA 95448
  707-433-4906

Please note that there are many places and companies from which you can purchase art supplies. We have listed places that we deal with on a regular basis to prepare for our presentations. You may find that you can purchase some or all of these supplies at a teacher supply store or an arts and crafts store in your area, or through mail-order catalogs.

At the time of publication, every effort was made to insure the accuracy of the information included in this book. However, we cannot guarantee that the agencies and organizations mentioned will continue to operate or to maintain these current locations.